The Great Platypus Caper & Other Hilarious Misadventures:
An Unreliable Autobiography

JEFF HILLARY

Published under license by:
Nowadays Orange Productions LLC
www.nowadaysorange.com

:

DEDICATION

I have long claimed that my parents are two of the most supportive people I've ever known. They backed every flight of fancy I've ever had (except the ones that might have gotten me killed). I'm pretty sure if I told them tomorrow I wanted to be an astronaut, they'd buy me a space suit for my birthday. Thank you both. This book is only possible because of the life you let me have.

This book is also dedicated to my friends, those of you that choose to be a part of my life, even though you don't have to be. Thank you for each and every adventure we've shared, and to the ones we haven't had yet. I'm very lucky to have you all in my life. I'd especially like to thank Gary, Princess, and Jess for putting up with me as long as they have.

Lastly, this book is dedicated to the memory of my friend Daniel. He was as close as a brother and as loving as a friend could be. While I will always deeply treasure the stories we shared together, I will forever mourn the adventures we never got to have.

CONTENTS

JEFF HILLARY

Prologue: Where Did I Go Wrong?

I've long felt that the greatest tragedy of my life is how unprepared I was for reality. All the books, games, and movies I enjoyed growing up promised me grand adventures. While life can often be an adventure, and this collection of stories proves that mine has had quite a few, I expected a more literal interpretation.

I spent my youth prepared to be magically whisked away to another land where I was a prophesied hero, and I had to lead an oppressed kingdom to victory over a tyrannical ruler (who was probably an evil wizard, or a dragon) and all I had to help me from my world was a yo-yo, which the natives of this magical land had never seen before. I'm actually still a little miffed this never happened. I could have overcome overwhelming odds, met new allies, made the epic speech about friendship that inspired our final victory, and finally turned down my place of honour in the kingdom to return home.

Actually, that last part always bothered me. Why does the hero always choose to return home? Seriously, you want to go from being a hero of the realm back to your job as a bag boy at the local grocery store while trying to make rent so you can finish putting yourself through college? Screw that, bring on the accolades and groupies!

I never did learn how to properly wield a sword, but I swing a mean baseball bat. And besides, these adventures never required the hero to be formally trained in a particular discipline. If you were good at video games, you got whisked away to a land where life WAS a video game. If you liked reading, then inevitably you were the only person capable of reading the notes left from an ancient civilization that unlocked the key to victory. All you had to do was be YOU, and victory was sure to follow.

I used to lay in bed at night and pretend to be a hero who could travel between realities, a hero who could go into any book I'd read, or game I'd play. Once there I could participate in the stories, slay the evil, get the girl, all the good stuff. Of course in that case, instead of staying or going home, I'd just head on to the next adventure. Somewhere out there, in the landscape of imagination, some version of me is spending all of eternity going from one grand adventure to another. I secretly hope someday I'll get to meet him. Hell, maybe he'd even be willing to trade places with me for a while, the guy probably needs a vacation.

The problem with all of these stories, and the ideas they give a young man, is that reality is far from that exciting. In our reality, you get a job as a teenager, and you keep having a job until you retire as an old man. Most of the money you earn from that job will go to pay the bills that keep you alive. Things you have to have, like food, a place to live, and of course the internet. Seriously, if tomorrow they figured out a way to make money unimportant, so many people would never work again. It's all a very far cry from saving a princess, slaying a dragon, or becoming a great sorcerer.

Now, as I grew older and wiser, I realized that real life was an adventure too, if we looked at it just the right way. Instead of finding some long lost artifact, we hunt for happiness and joy. We still make allies along the way, we call them friends. We slay beasts as we go, self-doubt, pity, loneliness, jealousy. In the end we can declare a victory, as we look back over our life and realize that we have lived a life we are proud of. We may not always like our job, but our job isn't our whole life. And if we pick your friends well, we can totally make those over-the-top friendship speeches that always seem to ensure victory. How exciting or enjoyable our life is, is entirely up to us. Never let anyone take that from you.

Although I still think I'd make a rockin' Legendary Hero of Prophecy, just in case there are any magical kingdoms out there looking to recruit new talent.

But even with all of that, there comes a time in a man's life where he has to honestly stop and take a look at himself. This is rarely a good idea, and it never ends well. I, like many people, spend the majority of my life in a haze of shameless egotism to avoid exactly this kind of confrontation with reality.

Recently however, I slipped, and took a long look at myself in the mirror. I'm 28, overweight, I live with my parents, and despite occasionally working on film sets, I'm essentially unemployed. This can't be the way my life was supposed to turn out. I understand that I'm never going to be called upon to slay dragons, or right great wrongs, but surely I'm capable of living a productive and relatively self-sustaining life.

What happened? We all start out with potential. When we're kids we're all told that we can grow up to be anything we want to be. At what point did I decide I wanted to be an unemployed fat bum mooching off my parents when I was almost 30? I swear I never saw that at career day. And let's not forget my love life...actually, it's probably better if we do.

Somewhere along the line, I messed up. Somehow my life jumped off the rails and crashed, leaving behind the remains of my self-respect and dignity. There has to be a way to fix this, it can't be too late to turn myself around and start heading towards a reasonable life goal. I have to be able to rid myself of this feeling that time is marching ever onward, and I'm just spinning my wheels.

The only thing I can do is look back over the memorable events of my life, and try to determine where I jumped the rails, and I'm taking you with me.

Maybe between the two of us we can sort this out.

The Sock Story

This story takes place, as so many great stories often do, when I moved into my first apartment. If nothing else, I feel it will properly illuminate how horribly unprepared I was for real life. I had moved into this place with a coworker of mine and a girl who lived on our couch (the actual arrangement was a lot more complicated and murky than that, but that's not the story you're here for).

I moved into this apartment the first semester of college, and it was my very first taste of living on my own, with two other people. Ok, perhaps it's better to say that it was my first time living with people who weren't related to me. Daniel, my co-worker, will feature in many more stories. Stacy, the girl, probably will not. There are three facts necessary to fully understanding this story, two of which I shall reveal now, the third will be revealed as it was to me.

Fact One: my mother is a very loving woman, although possibly a little crazy. And as it was my very first trip out in to the scary and frightening real world (a whole 30 minutes from my parents house) she wanted to be as supportive as possible. Thus she did my laundry for me. This was helpful as I'd never really done my own laundry, and I pictured my first attempt quickly becoming a Three Stooges film with only one stooge (i.e. ME). Years later I did teach myself how to do laundry, with surprisingly few injuries, and my mother was proud.

Fact Two: in between moving out of her last place and moving into our new place Stacy had packed all of her worldly possessions, and most importantly all her worldly clothing into her car for a couple weeks. It was broken into. Stacy ran the local Rocky Horror Picture Show Shadowcast (which I promise we will address in future stories, don't worry) and appealed to everyone to donate to her any clothes they could. What she received were the clothes that even Rocky Horror freaks refused to wear. To better help you picture what I'm talking about, know that a couple weeks later she was assumed to be a prostitute while walking down a street one day. This is not due to her demeanor, as she's quite a lovely person really. This confusion was due entirely to her crazy hodgepodge crack-whore dumpster-diving style wardrobe that had been donated to her.

And now our story begins.

As the weeks go by, I begin to notice that I'm running out of socks. It's an odd problem, and one I'd never encountered before. It was such a gradual process that it took quite some time for me to even be sure it was happening, but when I finally realized that I only had two pairs of socks I knew something was up. My first assumption was that Stacy was stealing my socks, and I didn't begrudge her that, considering that her entire wardrobe was a malfunction. So I went out to Wal-Mart and purchased myself some more socks.

A few months go by, and I am again down to two pairs of socks. Only this time Stacy was no longer living at the apartment. Daniel swore he did not touch my socks, and my search for magical sock-stealing pixies had come up completely empty. Remembering a book from my childhood I even checked the local flora to see if any of them looked like sock-eaters. They did not.

At this point I began addressing my concerns with my mother. Let me repeat again that my mother is a very loving woman, but she doesn't always trust that I know what I'm talking about. Her first suggestion was that all my socks were just tucked away in corners of my apartment and I wasn't looking hard enough. I assured her that I had SCOURED the apartment looking for socks (I left out the hunt for pixies or socknivorous plants). Her follow-up solution was that I must be hiding them.

Hiding my socks... from myself... in case I felt an overwhelming urge to wear them I suppose.

Twenty pairs of socks, hidden away in air vents and inside beloved stuffed animals. This is what my mother was picturing at my apartment. Or perhaps her deranged imagination roamed ever further than that, perhaps she thought I had some stashed in a safety deposit box, or that I'd opened a Swiss Sock Account overseas in order to protect my socks in an unstable economy. Whatever was occurring within her increasingly demented noggin, she was adamantly CONVINCED that my socks had NOT vanished, and I'd find them if I just looked harder, and ate more vegetables, and stood up straight. Those last two have ever been my mother's sure-fire solution to any and every problem I've ever had. If you add to that list "get out in the sun more", you've got my mother's cure for cancer.

By this point I had become OBSESSED with socks. No matter how many packs I bought, I always ended up with just two pair after a couple months. My mother denied anything was happening in the laundry, and Stacy was in another city entirely. I started having dreams about sleeping on a bed made entirely of socks. I would sit in class and just look at a cute girl's socks and think "Oh how lucky she is, she has SOCKS." I was alone in the desert just looking for a drop of water. A few poorly stitched together swathes of cotton were all I needed to get through my day. I'd even considered calling up Stacy and asking if I could borrow some clothes, that way I could start turning tricks for just a single pair of these modern marvels.

Finally, in a moment that could only be described as a fit of insanity, I went to my local Wal-Mart again (where I was now known as the sock guy, because I told my tale of woe to all that would listen) and bought an OBSCENE amount of socks. I STORMED to my parent's house and shoved them in my mother's face all the while screaming "THESE ARE SOCKS! I OWN THEM! THEY ARE MINE! THEY EXIST! THEY ARE NOT HIDDEN!"

My mother took my fit in stride, as she does most of my insanity. She simply looked at my fresh new wonderful GLORIOUS socks and said "Those aren't the kind of socks you wear. Those are the kind your father wears."

I don't think words can ever properly describe what went through my mind at that moment. Everything simply clicked. My anger evaporated, and I was very briefly left with a complete and total understanding of the universe. I believe I may even have seen the face of God. I understood everything. I hadn't been crazy all this time. It all made sense. All I'd been lacking was one tiny, almost insignificant fact.

Fact Three: For the past several months my father's sock drawer had become overflowing full. For no reason he could figure out, he now had to use TWO sock drawers just to contain all his socks, even though he wasn't buying any. He mentioned this to my mother several times, but she had no explanation. In all likelihood, she accused him of not really knowing how many socks he had to begin with, and that he was being silly for thinking he was acquiring more of these tiny little treasures.

To reiterate, while I was spending months yelling at my mother about how my socks were disappearing, my father was complaining to her that he was accumulating an ungodly amount of socks for no reason. The only person in this entire story who KNEW both sides of this issue, the woman doing the laundry for all the relevant parties, the woman who was unshakably certain that this entire fiasco was somehow MY fault, was my mother.

This became my favourite story to tell for a very long time, especially when people would wonder about why I have a deep and abiding appreciation for good socks, or why I have so many pairs of socks. With every telling of this story, it grows in length. I think if I tell it just a couple more times I can make a feature-length film out of it.

My mother, of course, always hates me telling this story, because she feels like it casts her in a poor light. She has said many times that I never tell HER side of the story.

One day I sat down with her, and very calmly asked her for her side of the story. I asked for her side of how she spent months listening to me complain about my vanishing socks, and my father complain about how his socks were reproducing like tribbles, and never put the two of them together. I BEGGED her to explain her side to me. I pleaded for the illumination to finally understand what must have been going on in that well-meaning but incredibly mixed up brain of hers. In the name of fairness, I will now share with you what she told me.

She paused for 30 seconds, gathered her thoughts, looked me straight in the eye, and said "I'm sorry."

Suffice to say, I never groan when I get socks for Christmas, and neither should you. You never know how precious they are until they're gone.

The Other Sock Story

I realize it's particularly brave to start a collection of stories talking about socks. Writing about something so audacious, so edgy, this early on could easily alienate my audience. Millions of people could read that first story and realize that this collection of memories is far too rich for their blood, and go find something a little more laid back and easy. But I'm such a wild rebel that I'm going to follow that up with another story about socks, or in this case a sock.

First, the background. In the previous story I mentioned a Rocky Horror Picture Show Shadowcast. Henceforth we will just call it Rocky. If for any reason I need to bring up the Sylvester Stallone boxing movie, I promise to point out that we're talking about a different Rocky.

For those of you who don't know what a Shadowcast is, it's when a group of people come together and act out a movie, in a movie theater, while the movie is playing on a large screen behind them. To some of you this probably sounds like an incredibly absurd idea. Congratulations, you're sane. For those of us in Rocky though, sanity was a nuisance we rarely encountered.

I spent approximately three years involved with Rocky, first as a regular audience member every Saturday night, and then on cast (I played Eddie and Riff-Raff for those who might care).

Now, when you put on the same show every Saturday night for mostly the same audience for multiple years, you have to find ways to spice it up on occasion. One such way was to do theme shows. One such theme show was the Disney show, where everyone dressed up as Disney characters and acted out the films (completely raping your childhood in the process). The Halloween show was always fun, because all bets were off. I've seen Frank-N-Furter played as a Pregnant Nun (who gave birth in the dinner scene) while Brad and Janet were Jack Skellington and Sally.

The theme show that will be the focal point of our story is the lingerie show. Now, Rocky is at all times very sexually charged. It's not just the movie on the screen, it's all of us gathered together dancing around in corsets and high heels (even the guys on occasion). So the lingerie show is really just an excuse to maximize the titillation. With this in mind, I decided to be funny (or at least my best imitation of funny). While everyone else was going to Victoria's Secret (or more often her slutty STD-riddled, jailbait sister Fredrick's of Hollywood), I had devised an entirely different plan. I showed up that night dressed in a thick bathrobe, and some humorous boxer shorts. I explained to everyone that it was male lingerie. It's the kind of thing your dad would wear when he wanted to feel sexy.

But that was only the start of my dastardly plan.

Near the end of the show my character was supposed to change into a skimpy spacesuit with fishnets. I will to this day proclaim that my calves look AMAZING in fishnets, and that's not something a lot of straight guys get to claim. However fishnets weren't on the menu this evening. I had decided for my finale to come out wearing nothing but a sock.

Mind you, it wasn't on my foot, it was a strategically placed sock. I'll try to avoid being too graphic, but there is some information you need to have at this point. When attempting to wear a sock strategically, there is only one way to do it. You place the most obvious part of your anatomy in the sock of course, but then you must also tuck in the two other pieces of anatomy. This prevents you from exposing your anatomy to the world, and helps keep the sock on. Also, it keeps your anatomy warm on those cold lonely nights.

This may be a good time to point out that the theater we were performing in was a very upscale facility. Glass chandelier, hard wood floors, film festivals coming through on a regular basis, and I'm running (very carefully) around the building wearing a sock.

Now, this seemed like a hilarious idea when I came up with it, but I know me pretty well (I've been around me most of my life after all), and I knew I was going to chicken out at the last second. So I took all of my clothes, and handed them to a rather large security guard who worked for the show. I told him to take all my clothes and throw them in the theater. Under NO circumstances was he to return them to me, no matter what I said.

With about a minute before I need to go out in front of over 200 people wearing nothing but a sock, I start freaking out. I began threatening a man at least thrice my size with physical violence if he didn't go and fetch my clothes forthwith. He threatened to throw my sock into the theater as well. And then it was time for my entrance, and the professional actor that I am could not miss my cue. So out I went.

The audience thought it was kind of funny at first, but it wasn't until I slowly walked in front of all of them that the full effect sunk in. As row by row of people got to see my butt wagging in the breeze, and realized I really was wearing nothing but a single sock, secured in place only by my anatomy, the laughter built rather rapidly.

A few more notes on this performance. Rocky is a musical, and usually we sing along with our characters in the film (you don't have to, but it's considered better if you do). At this point in the film my character is singing some VERY high-pitched notes. For those of you who don't know, when a man is singing VERY high-pitched notes, things tend to shift. The things I'm referencing are the very last things in the world that I wanted shifting at this moment, the things that were in fact, holding the sock on. I quickly realized that I needed to abandon singing along tonight, or abandon what little dignity I had left. Later there is a moment where my character takes a very large and exaggerated step to the right. As that moment arrived

I had a moment of fear that was clearly shared by the audience. Such a largely exaggerated movement could liberate me of the one thing I valued above all else at this moment, my sock. In unison, as if someone had held up a cue card, the entire audience yelled "NO DON'T". Once again professionalism kicked in, and I made the step. It was very nearly the last step I ever made.

Oddly none of my cast mates could look me in the face, and there were a lot of people having issues keeping from busting out laughing. Haven't they ever heard of being professional? I mean really. You'd think that someone wearing nothing but a sock was somehow shocking or abnormal. After the show, comfortably ensconced in my bathrobe once more, a young lady from the audience approached me and asked if she could have the sock.

I was perplexed. I tried to explain that the sock had another sock that it went with, and that they were meant to be together. If I gave her this sock, then I would have a completely worthless sock sitting at home. She insisted upon her desire for the sock, and offered me $5 with which to go buy a new pair. I conceded, and even signed the sock upon her request. The next week I was rewarded with a picture of the sock hanging proudly on her wall.

Tragically we may never know the true fate of the sock that lost its partner that night. It lived for a time in my trunk, but I haven't seen it in some time. I'm forced to assume that it escaped late one night, and even today it's travelling across the country seeking its long lost partner.

My infamy was short-lived however, as a couple months later the actor playing the eponymous character of

Rocky Horror performed his entire part naked.

All in all, another normal evening at Rocky.

It is worth noting, that many many years later I received a very curious email. Inside this email were several photographs of me dancing around in a sock that fateful night. High-quality photographs. Very high-quality digital photographs. At first I was disgusted, "oh man, what the hell was I thinking!?" Then I noticed how much thinner I was back then (still not thin enough to make me look the least bit appealing in these photos, but thinner than I am now). And then I promptly saved them all to my hard drive to threaten my friends with from time to time.

I am a little concerned with the fact that somewhere out there is a man with a hard drive full of these photos. I'm pretty sure this means I can't run for President….then again, considering some of the Presidents we've had, maybe I should make them my campaign poster.

Vote Jeff, when you're tired of candidates with shame and dignity!

My Imaginary Friend Russ

All of the friends I've made over the years have been unique, quirky, or downright bizarre. Over the years I've simply begun explaining my friends as the Isle of Misfit People. I've got an affable giant, a neurotic perfectionist, a polyamorous musician, a terminally shy philosophy professor in training, a complete douchebag, an introvert furry graphic designer, a girl who hates me (yet claims I'm her only friend), and an imaginary friend, among countless others.

Yes, I have an imaginary friend named Russ. Now, some of you may think it odd that a 28-year-old man has an imaginary friend (and if you don't think it odd, please seek help) but in my defense, he wasn't always imaginary. He used to be a real flesh-and-blood live boy, with an amazing talent.

Russ and I met in my very first class in college. I was bored to tears by the lecture going on, so I opened up my laptop and played my favourite video game of all time,

Earthbound. Russ, a complete stranger to me at that point, leaned over to see what I was playing. Upon seeing Earthbound in all its emulated glory, he squealed with delight (yes, Russ is a squealer) and told me it was his favourite game ever. And in that moment a life long bond was forged.

Now, Russ is a great guy, and everyone loves having him around. He is completely fabulous (in every meaning of the word). But he's also, and I phrase this as nicely as I can, a tremendous flake. He has a habit of not returning calls, texts, or emails. Anytime he promises to be somewhere, it's a 50-50 chance that he shows. If he doesn't show, you won't hear from him for WEEKS about why. Actually, you just won't hear from him for weeks, you'll never know why.

I've been friends with Russ for about 10 years now, and about half that time he's just been....gone. He vanishes for months, or even years, before springing back up. At first it was irritating, but over time I grew to accept it as a part of who he is. However, over the years I've made many friends who hear me talk about Russ, but never actually meet the man. Some of my newer friends are convinced he doesn't really exist. Some of my older friends who have actually met him are even starting to doubt they ever met him. Pictures taken of the elusive Russ are beginning to be declared Photoshop jobs. Until one day I officially declared him to be my imaginary friend, and everyone took that in stride.

Now, the more astute of you out there are probably thinking the same thing my mother did. My mother is one of nature's skeptics, and there are times I wonder if she's ever believed anything anyone has told her. While a supportive woman, to be sure, she can also think the absolute worst of people from time to time. Her theory is that Russ doesn't like me at all, but he's just too shy to be up front about it.

If you believe like my mother, you are wrong sir (or madam)! Let me tell you why. After many years of this I began to suspect the same thing myself. And in a fit of anger told him that he no longer needed to worry about avoiding me, we could simply cease being friends and he need never hear from me again.

He apologized profusely, and BEGGED for another chance. I offered him a way out, and he refused to take it, instead pleading to stay. He was a very attentive and reliable friend after that, for about a month.

Typically when Russ vanishes, my solution is to randomly show up on his doorstep and wait for him to get home from work. Upon seeing me he proclaims how delighted he is to see me, and we hang out and play video games. Russ is my preferred Player 2 in almost any game.

Now we arrive at Russ's remarkable ability. Russ is the greatest AND worst video game player ever. I realize some of you reading this may not be video gamers yourselves, so I'll try to keep this simple.

The best example of this, and the most iconic, centered around a game called Wind Waker. Now Wind Waker was an older game at this point, but I was showing my friend Princess how to play it (yes, I have a friend named Princess, I also have a friend who's a werewolf, just deal with it). Russ came over to watch Princess play this game that she'd never played before. Russ and I had both beaten this game many years before.

In the game is a fairly simple puzzle. You walk up to a giant ball, pick it up, carry it a short distance, and set it down. Easy, right? Now, you can HIT the ball instead of picking it up, and it'll roll for a couple seconds before it shatters, and reappears in it's original spot. Princess did as I believe every gamer did. She walked up to the ball, picked it up, and moved it. At this moment Russ cried out a phrase that has long since become a catchphrase amongst my friends, "YOU CAN PICK THAT UP!?".

It turns out Russ spent DAYS hitting that ball around, trying to get it where it needed to be before it shattered and he had to start again. A method to solve the problem that I am positive the designers of the game never imagined anyone doing. Entire DAYS were spent whacking this ball around because Russ didn't realize it could simply be lifted.

Allow me to share another quick example in the same game. There is a puzzle sequence where you have to swing and jump from rope to rope to rope, but it's in a 3D environment, and sometimes the ropes aren't where you need them to be. The obvious solution is to stop swinging on your rope, turn a little bit, start swinging again, and jump to the next rope. Russ never realized you could stop and turn. Once again DAYS were spent trying to figure out how to line up his jumps so that he could finish this remarkably simple part of the game.

So he possesses almost NO intuitive game playing abilities. He frequently fails to see how a simple puzzle is meant to be solved. So he's the worst video game player ever. BUT, he never stops, he ALWAYS beats these games. He finds solutions a thousand times more complicated, solutions none of us mere mortals could EVER achieve. He's like a freaking machine. Nothing will stop him from beating these games in the most ridiculously difficult manner possible. He's the greatest video game player ever.

So the next time you or your friends are playing a game, and somebody misses a completely obvious game mechanic, or completely fails to understand what they are doing, and someone else points it out to them, it is your duty to proclaim "YOU CAN PICK THAT UP!?", for Russ, my imaginary friend.

JEFF HILLARY

My Friend the Axe Wielding Maniac

Speaking of odd friends, remember Daniel? Daniel was my coworker turned first roommate, turned best friend, turned heterosexual life mate. By this point you also know a little bit about Rocky, which Daniel was also in with me.

One very important part of Rocky is the aftermath. See, the show starts at midnight on a Saturday, and there's usually hanging out afterwards, plus it's a fairly intense performance. You may well wonder how running around acting out a movie in front of that same movie could be intense. You have no idea.

The first performance I ever gave was as Eddie. For those that don't know the film, Eddie's a pretty sweet gig. You come out about halfway through the movie, have a four minute musical number, and then get killed. For that four minutes you are like unto God. You are the coolest kid in school, you play a pretend saxophone, you swing dance and lift a girl up over your head, you then pretend to make-out with that girl on the floor, and then run around until you get an over-the-top death scene.

The first time I played Eddie, I thought I was going to die, literally. After I got off stage my heart was pounding harder than it ever had before. I could hear it in my ears even as I gasped for breath. Part of it was the stage fright, part of it was the adrenaline rush, and part of it was just having lifted a girl up over my head and holding her there, plus singing at the top of my lungs the entire time.

I knew I just needed to get a drink of water from the fountain and calm down for a few minutes. The only issue was, my heart was pumping so hard that my pulse actually knocked the water out of my mouth before I could swallow it.

It's at that moment I realized my first performance in Rocky was going to kill me. A quiet calm came over me as I realized that I was about to die. My heart was literally going to explode in my chest, and I would die at the age of 18 while dressed as a character from The Rocky Horror Picture Show. I pictured my parents frantically trying to come up with a different story to tell the neighbors.

In all honesty, that calm that came over me is probably what saved my life. My heart slowed down, I drank some water, and did it all over again every Saturday after that for years. My heart never decided to act up quite like that again, apparently it liked being in show business.

If that's what a 4 minute part can do to you, imagine being one of the main characters.

We also lived about 45 minutes away from where we

performed Rocky. The short version is that coming home at 6am from Rocky, you are the most tired you've EVER been in your life. I've stayed up for days at a time for college, I've slept in my car for weeks at a time working crew on movie sets, and I even once had a 24 hour work day shooting a music video. None of that has ever compared to how exhausted I was every Sunday morning.

Another important piece of information is that our first apartment was pretty bad. Very possibly the worst part was the paper-thin walls, allowing every sound in the neighborhood for miles around to sound as if it were occurring INSIDE MY HEAD!

As a brief side story about that apartment by the way, one day they decided to increase safety by installing new lights outside the apartment building, right next to the windows in our bedrooms. These lights were about twice as bright as THE FREAKING SUN. It was impossible to tell when it was night time in our apartment. Daniel and I dealt with the problem as men do, we tacked up some blankets over the window. See, women would have gone and gotten window dressings, maybe blackout curtains. But men, we're very simple creatures. A couple of pushpins and a nice yellow blanket, and problem solved. Of course the lights were VERY powerful, and all hanging up the blanket did was make my entire room yellow hued every night...but it was better than Daniel's room. He used a red blanket. Every night his room looked like the setting for a horror film.

Anyway, back to the story at hand. Daniel and I arrive home one Sunday morning after Rocky. Daniel immediately passes out, while I struggle to fall asleep (no matter how exhausted I am, I sleep poorly, a topic for another time). Fifteen minutes after Daniel has passed out, a large group of children begin playing loudly outside our windows. Thanks to the lovely quality of the building, they might as well have been playing in our bedrooms, it was amazingly loud and crystal clear. That's right, our apartment pioneered HD technology, bringing you the best possible audio quality in other people's children playing whilst you yearn for sleep.

There are two versions of what happened next. Daniel's version, and the actual version. Out of fairness to Daniel, I'll start with his version.

Daniel, awoken by this ruckus, grabs the nearest menacing object he can find. Being a collector of medieval weapons, this meant he grabbed a Scottish axe. It's worth noting that Daniel (and I for that matter) had a tendency to sleep only in his boxer shorts. The shorts in question on this particular morning had little hearts on them. So Daniel, garbed in his heart boxers and ought else but his Scottish axe, runs out of our apartment and to a balcony overlooking the kids. Raising the axe above his head in a threatening manner he yells "Hey you stupid kids! I'm trying to sleep in here! Shut the hell up or I'll come down there!"

That is Daniel's version, the wrong version. You see, Daniel was a great deal groggier than me, since he had actually been asleep (albeit very briefly) before this happened. I witnessed events with a (relatively) clear head, and what follows is nothing but the truth.

His actions and wardrobe, and even weapon of choice, were all exactly as previously stated. However, when it came time to yell at the children, what he actually yelled   was "Hoogaboogaboogashumhumazamanannahuzunagalibaheze!" (That was harder to spell than you'd think).

The ending to both versions is the same. The children, confronted with a crazed white man wearing heart boxers and wielding an axe while incoherently yelling at them, reacted as I think any of us would. They ran away screaming.

Daniel went back to his room, a hero in my heart, and slept the sleep of the just and righteous.

Oddly enough, we never really had to deal with playing children on Sunday morning anymore. I like to pretend that the kids shared stories amongst themselves. Hushed and urgent tales of a crazed Viking (Daniel's hair had a definite Viking flair to it) who would run out of the fog (or an apartment) if they had too much fun in the morning. He'd swoop down with his axe and yell at you in the Devil's own language. If you didn't heed his warning, he'd swallow your soul.

Or perhaps they chose to play at an apartment complex where the adults wore clothes, and didn't have axes.

Could go either way really.

Freezer Burn

I would like to start out being on record as stating that it is not my fault we had a dead rat in our freezer for over a year.

I'm actually tempted to let that be the entire story. You have to admit, it's a pretty awesome sentence. But, I suppose I can provide further illumination into the situation.

Early on in our first apartment Stacy (remember Stacy? She was the poor girl who was basically forced to dress as a hobo hooker for a while) decided that we needed pets. So she went out and got a rabbit, and a hairless rat. Trust me, we asked her why she decided to get a hairless rat. She claimed to have gotten the hairless rat because it was the ugliest pet in the pet store. If you knew Stacy, that was as logical an answer as you were ever going to get.

Neither Daniel nor I felt obligated to take care of these critters, they were Stacy's pets. We weren't really consulted in the purchase of them. This may be what caused them to die in relatively short order. Stacy, dissatisfied with life on our couch (which really is a much longer story that may be told one day) was spending more and more time at what I assume was her boyfriend's apartment.

The rat died first, probably of terminal ugliness. Daniel and I called her and offered to bury it, because we didn't want a dead rat to ruin the ambiance of our complete dump of an apartment. Stacy quickly told us NO. She voiced concern that I would bury it in some bizarre pagan ritual. In my defense, I've never been a part of any pagan ritual, bizarre or otherwise. Daniel, who had quite a thing for Stacy at that time (probably because of her unique and quirky wardrobe) promised that we would not bury it until Stacy got back later that week.

This left us with an obvious problem, of the decomposing kind. Luckily I have occasions where I am a GENIUS, and one of those moments struck me just then. I took a Pringles can, emptied out all the chips, and put the rat inside it. We then put the Pringles can in our freezer. Air tight and frozen, problem solved. Hell, we weren't just your average college students dealing with a dead hairless rat, we were trailblazers in the field of cryogenics.

A few days later we were having a party, and Daniel and I both were concerned that someone at the party would open the freezer, see the Pringles can in there, and think to themselves "Oh my God! Frozen Pringles! My favourite!" and then they would open them, and disaster would ensue. We thought this would be pretty funny. Then we realized it could be a hot chick who did it, and then she wouldn't want to have sex with either of us. Freeze-dried rats being a famous anti-aphrodisiac. In another flash of genius I grabbed a nearby crayon (why two college guys had an orange crayon randomly laying around in their apartment is simply one of those great mysteries of life) and wrote on the Pringles can "NOT FOOD". Worried that this might not deter a particularly inebriated frozen Pringles connoisseur, I decided to further add "DO NOT EAT".

Now, Stacy came and went several times from the apartment the next couple months, but never had time to address the dead rat issue. So it continued to freeze. The longer it was in the freezer, the less any of us cared about it. It's actually interesting how quickly a person becomes used to something like a dead frozen hairless rat in the freezer. They should really do a study about that sort of thing.

The bunny also died. Being somewhat larger we had to put it in a shoe box in the freezer. Now, you might be surprised to learn this, but a shoe box isn't air tight, and it's gross to put an animal in your freezer if they aren't in an airtight container. How do a couple of genius college guys solve a conundrum like this? Duct tape.

Quickly Daniel (choosing to be the sensible one of us) decided this was ridiculous. In Daniel's mind, a frozen dead hairless rat in a Pringle can was perfectly acceptable, but a dead bunny in a duct-taped shoe box was crossing the line. So he took the shoe box to his parents' house and hid it under a giant pile of leaves. Another problem sorted out. We would often speculate (but never dare ask) what happened when his step-father encountered the box in the process of his normal yard care duties. Truly it's a mystery that will eat at me until the end of my days.

When Stacy finally moved out, the rat had officially become a resident of the freezer, and the thought of removing it no longer crossed any of our minds. Occasionally one of us would look at the other and say "We have a dead rat in the freezer". We'd laugh for a while and go back to whatever we were doing. Every so often I'd try to think of a way to extort rent money from the rat.

The rat was not the only horror of our fridge. When we first moved in I bought a half gallon of milk. I drank about half of it, and then got distracted by something shiny and forgot it existed for a couple weeks. By then it was well past its expiration date, but I didn't feel like throwing it out. Daniel certainly wasn't going to throw out my mess (especially since he was rarely willing to clean up his own). That milk stayed in the fridge until we moved out over a year later, a true testament to male stubbornness. By that point we affectionately referred to it as The Cheese. I'll spare you a description, but I'm pretty sure it was gaining sentience, and hair.

Oh yeah, and when we moved out, we did leave the dead rat in the freezer for the next people (my vote to place it in an air vent was firmly denied). We figured it was the least we could do. I seriously hope whoever moved in after us did not open that can. I imagine it would be like that scene at the end of Raiders of the Lost Ark…faces melting in horror.

Although, if they did open it, I hope they paid heed to my written warnings, "NOT FOOD, DO NOT EAT", because I have absolutely no idea what a 2 year old dead frozen rat looks like. But somewhere out there is someone who might.

Ebony, Ivory, and the KKK

For the next story we expand our cast of characters by two. First, Princess, who was briefly mentioned earlier, and secondly, Maurice. Princess is an itty-bitty, very pale redheaded girl. She's remarkably intelligent and driven. Graduated with a double major from college in about two years, and is currently top of her class at law school. She also has a tendency to very clearly speak her mind, without sugar coating. Often she speaks it without taking into account the audience she's speaking to either.

Maurice is a friendly giant. The man is about seven feet tall, admittedly on the heavy side, and black. Now normally I wouldn't bring up his race, because in all honesty I don't give a crap about race or any of the other bullshit we use to separate ourselves into little groups that can hate the other groups. I find all of that incredibly tedious and a waste of time. I dislike people based on their individual character, not on factors such as race, sexual orientation, religion, or favourite cheese.

Point of fact, an old acquaintance recently contacted me (I used to lift her above my head at Rocky ten years previously, funny how these things are all connected) and asked if I knew any black guys she could use in a television show she was casting. It actually took me ten minutes to remember that Maurice was black, I'm really just not used to thinking in those terms. The only reason I brought up his race is because his race has a vital impact on this story.

This story is notable because I am positive that nothing like it has ever happened anywhere else in the history of the world. I had a large number of friends over that evening (no, I won't bother naming or describing them all). At the end of the evening I convinced Maurice to tell his KKK story, because it's my favourite story of his. I've made him tell it multiple times but it never gets old. What follows is my poor attempt to paraphrase his magnum opus.

Apparently Maurice and some friends were traveling the back roads of some hick southern state. (Hey, I'm an 11th generation Texan, I get to point out that there are some hicks in the South.) On this trip they notice a large gathering in the woods, and it looks like a rocking good party, so they go to investigate. It's worth noting that all of Maurice's friends in this instance are white. When they get to the party it slowly dawns on Maurice that he is the only black person there. It takes a few minutes, but after a few stares and angry mutters he further realizes that this is a Ku Klux Klan gathering. So they killed him.

Ok, obviously not, because he was alive to tell the story. They were probably too scared to attack him directly. He was most likely the largest black man they'd ever seen. It was probably like seeing Godzilla walking into an animal control convention. In fact I promise at least one of those backwards hicks thought "we're going to need a bigger boat."

Maurice, being the charming talker that he is, strikes up a conversation with the racists, in an attempt to calm them down so he can make good his escape. What follows are, to the best of my memory, his exact words.

"Ok look, you guys want all us black people to go back to Africa right? Well, the problem with that is that we've been here so long that most of us have never even seen Africa. I was born in Chicago, my mother was born in Chicago. There's just way too many of us here now for you to ship us all back. But I have a solution for you.

You've got 4 time zones right? Just give us one of those. The next time we have one of our regular meetings I'll tell all the other black people that we're all moving into one time zone, and staying there."

To which the Klansmen were reported to have said "Hey, this feller (not the real word they used, the one they used had a lot more g's in it) has a point. He's pretty smart, for a feller (again, my word, not theirs)."

Maurice continued. "But you need to think about this first. If you give us the Eastern time zone, you lose New York, and that's where a lot of your television comes from. Every channel will basically become BET, plus we'll have Florida. You'd have to tell all your grandparents to pack up and retire somewhere else.

Now, you could give us the Central time zone, but that'll give us control over most of your farmland. You'd be putting us directly in control of feeding all of you guys. I mean, we wouldn't mind, but you'd need to be sure you were ok with eating the food we picked. We'd probably have to touch it and everything.

Now, you aren't giving us the Mountain time zone, it's just too cold. I can't take that to all the other black people and get them to agree to it. Seriously, when's the last time you saw a black person skiing? It's just not going to happen.

That just leaves you with the Pacific time zone. That gives us California. More importantly L.A. and Hollywood. This basically means that you can get used to Tyler Perry and the Wayans Brothers, because they're going to be the stars of every movie for the rest of time.

You guys just pick which one of those you can live without, and let me know."

Thereafter Maurice was accepted, and even drank a few beers with the Klan. He even claims to have run into a couple of Klansmen years later, and asked them if they'd picked a time zone yet. The Klansmen had no clue what he was talking about, and Maurice was very upset. It's really a crying shame to learn that the Klan doesn't have the same organization skills as the entire black race. So much for claiming to be superior.

Now, here comes the historical part. After Maurice tells this story to my friends, Princess chimes up "Let me tell you something good about the Klan though!"

I defy you to find another place in history where a large black man tells a story about the KKK and how he was in danger of getting lynched (of course, to lynch

Maurice they'd have needed a heavy duty tow cable and a skyscraper), and an upper middle class, tiny pale redheaded chick's very next words are defending the Klan. I DEFY YOU. Now, to be completely fair to Princess (and because I promised never to tell this story without fairly representing her side of it), here is her brief story that followed.

Apparently her grandfather was in the Klan. Not that being in the Klan isn't bad enough, but apparently he was a complete bastard as well, and nobody liked him much. As a testament to his bastardosity he would regularly beat his wife and kids (it could have just been one or the other, I misremember). That's right, he was a racist who had enough hate in his heart to also beat white people. When the Klan found out about this, they beat the living daylights out of him and he never raised a hand to them again.

So in Princess' defense, she had a perfectly decent point, but nobody else on the planet would have phrased it the way she did, at the time she did, in front of the people she did. But in her mind, there was nothing questionable about it. She had a point, she was going to make it, end of story.

That's why Princess is one of my favourite people ever.

Lycanthropy and Nudity

Now I've been holding off on this story because I felt I needed to establish trust ahead of time. Now that I've told you about me dancing around in a sock, perhaps you'll believe me when I say the following sentence. I had a friend who was a werewolf.

That's really another one of those sentences that should be an entire story.

I know it's a fantastic claim. I'm essentially saying that werewolves and possibly other mythological creatures actually exist in this world. Thanks to Twilight there are now legions of young girls desperately waiting to get accounts on emonsterharmony so they can date them.

It's an incredible claim, and I can't prove beyond a shadow of a doubt that he was in fact a werewolf, but I will present to you the facts at my disposal, and allow you to draw your own conclusions. Mind you, if your conclusions differ from mine, they are the wrong conclusions. However, I believe that everyone is entitled to their own opinion, even when it's the wrong one.

This goes way back to my first job as a teenager. I worked in a grocery store. It was there I met Daniel (who showed up in previous stories) and Kyle (who will show up in later stories).

In this store was an employee I now only think of as Werewolf. He had a proper name, I'm sure of it, but it's lost to the mists of time. I can't remember what caused me to think he was a lycanthrope, but something told me he had to be. I started calling him Werewolf long before the epic night I'm about to describe for you, and he never tried to correct me, so that is one strike against him to start.

Now, Daniel is a crucial part of the story. Daniel, Werewolf, and I all worked in different areas of the store, and had different schedules. This particular night Werewolf was going home before any of us. When he left, it was night time, and there was a full moon.

About an hour later Werewolf's dad came into the store, and went to Daniel's area (it was the customer service area, and the cash office). Werewolf Sr. tells Daniel that he is there to collect Werewolf's clothes, which had been left in the parking lot. Daniel non-plussed hands over a stack of clothes and Werewolf Sr. leaves. I will testify to those facts in court, because I witnessed them first-hand.

Now, it's not every day someone leaves ALL OF THEIR CLOTHES (that includes underwear) in a parking lot. So I asked Daniel if he knew any more about it. Apparently on a quick trip to his car for something, Daniel noticed all of Werewolves clothes in the parking lot, spread out in a line, underwear and all. Daniel picked them up, and was planning on giving them back to Werewolf the next day. However the sudden appearance of Werewolf Sr. made those plans obsolete.

My question was this: how does one leave all of their clothes in a line in the parking lot. And how does that kid's father come in to pick them up without any degree of shock or embarrassment on behalf of his child? Seriously, if this had somehow happened to my child, I'd be a little sheepish in asking for the clothes back from a complete stranger. I may also insinuate that my child was raised in a barn, or perhaps claim he was adopted (I'm adopted; I get to make those kinds of jokes).

Werewolf's story the next day when I asked was simple. He got off work, changed out of his work clothes in the parking lot, put them on top of his car to get in, forgot they were there and drove off. This is why when they were found they were strung out in a line in the parking lot. They simply flew off his car as he was traveling along.

At first glance it's a perfectly plausible story, sure, but I'm famous for always having more questions. The issue with this story is it requires him to be completely naked in the parking lot of an open and active grocery store. Something which I'm sure wouldn't have gone unnoticed. Surely if someone stripped down naked in the parking lot of a busy grocery store, the cops would have been called.

In the name of fairness (and potentially undoing my entire story) I should point out that later the next week I myself stripped completely naked in that parking lot to change clothes, but I was going to Rocky, and somehow forgot that I wasn't already there. At Rocky, such behavior is perfectly acceptable; Werewolf did not have this excuse. Also when I changed, it was around 11pm, when Werewolf changed it was around 8, more traffic.

Now, Daniel is the only person who knew Werewolf's real name, and I can't ask him anymore, so I can't track down Werewolf to press for more details. As I see it, there is only one logical conclusion that can be drawn from the facts at hand.

Werewolf, being young, was unprepared for the full moon. Maybe he worked later than he was planning, or maybe he just forgot it was that time of the month. He stepped outside, saw the moon, and began to wolf out. Quickly stripping out of his clothes as he ran to a more secluded location he transformed completely. His father, either being a lycanthrope himself, or at least aware of his son's condition, of course wouldn't be horribly shocked by having to go and get his son's clothes from the store.

Now, why do I believe people would have seen him strip down naked, but nobody called the police to claim they saw a werewolf in the grocery store parking lot?

Ok smarty pants, answer me this. You're walking into a grocery store and see a young man turn into a werewolf. Do you honestly tell anyone? You'd get locked up in a loony bin. And this was all before cameras had phones and videos on them. You'd keep that to yourself, or get therapy.

So somewhere out there is a werewolf, and I just hope he has fond memories of me. I also hope that publishing this story doesn't put me on some kind of werewolf black list. I don't want to have to start carrying silver with me during the full moon.

The Night I Went Blind

This title isn't meant to be a figure of speech, or even an exaggeration. This title 100% accurately depicts the events I'm about to share with you. There is only one new character for this story, Gertrude. I'd like to take a moment to point out that I've replaced the names of all my ex's in this book with old lady names, because it amuses me. Gertrude and I dated for a couple years, and for a while we were in Rocky together. We'd actually met at Rocky, which may tell you more than you'd like to guess about the type of person she is. In her defense though, I never had a complaint about her as a girlfriend. Even my friends who didn't like her didn't have anything negative to say about our relationship.

The setting? The drive home from Rocky. I have previously addressed how exhausted you are after Rocky, and that 45 minute drive home feels like it takes years. It's actually thanks to three years of driving home from Rocky well beyond the point of exhaustion that I can now confidently drive however long I want under any conditions without fear of falling asleep at the wheel. I've probably clocked more miles half asleep than I ever have awake.

Now, Gertrude and I had a very fair and simple division of labour to make that drive as pleasant as possible. Every week I would drive, and she would sleep in the passenger seat. It was a good arrangement, because...ummm...yeah that just sucked.

This particular night it was raining, and raining HARD. Luckily we were about the only car on the road. This is lucky because it was raining hard enough that I could barely see the road. I began driving by Braille. This is when you put your tires on top of the dividing line so you can feel it bump on the little safety thingies. I'm assuming that's what they are there for.

Now, I drive remarkably well in rain for a Texan. Most Texans see rain and just decide to live in their car on the side of the road for a couple weeks until they get over the whole mysterious "water from the sky" thing. And we're not even going to begin addressing the issue of Texans driving on ice or snow, the state just shuts completely down.

This is where our story takes a turn for the worse. I glanced off to the left, I don't know why, I'll never know why, the reason for this decision will always remain a mystery to me, but the consequences are something I'll never be able to forget. Just as I look over there I see a lightning bolt hit a giant transformer. After that all I see is blue. Baby blue. Undifferentiated, no shades or hues, it's solid blue. I'm going down the road at 60 miles an hour in treacherous weather, and I'm blind.

One of my greatest attributes is being calm in a crisis. I knew I couldn't start freaking out, because it'd wake up Gertrude and she'd start freaking out, and we'd crash, and we'd die. So I very gently reach over and wake her up. I explain to her very calmly that I need her to take the wheel of the vehicle and slowly move us onto the shoulder. I tell her I'm going to start gradually decelerating, and that everything will be fine. I honestly feel I should get some bonus points for thinking that quickly on my feet. Stuck blind by lightning, I don't swerve or slam on the brakes, I arrange for the passenger to slowly go for the shoulder while I gradually decelerate. Honestly, the more I think about it, the more I'd like a trophy or a plaque for that kind of intelligence under fire.

And here's where you get to learn a little bit of Gertrude's back-story. Not long before we began dating, she'd been in a very bad car wreck. She had metal in her leg, and some serious post-traumatic stress issues. It was not uncommon for her to start wigging out and crying if I turned a corner too fast, or bumped a curb. Once, with a car full of people, I actually had to pull over to the side of the road and calm her down after a car cut me off in traffic. She had issues with cars. So you can imagine her reaction to being woken up in the middle of a car ride home, when it's raining too hard to see more than a few feet in front of us, we're going sixty miles an hour, and the driver is blind. To say she begins freaking out is an understatement.

I can't recall her exact words, I was a little focused on my own personal crisis, but there was a lot of sobbing, high-pitched screeching, and the phrase "Oh my God" over and over again. Normally when she yelled something like this, it was under much more pleasant circumstances. These were not pleasant circumstances.

Now, I'm blind. And I can't help but having a thought flash through my head really quick.

I'd heard about a film called Blue, which is a documentary about a man dying of AIDS, and about two thirds of the way through the film the man goes blind, and all he can see is blue. The film itself represents this by having the last third of the film be a nice light blue, and all you can do is listen. This had me thinking that maybe all blind people see blue. It's not like they'd know it was blue, so they couldn't tell us. We assume they see black, but that's a pretty big assumption.

So with that racing through my mind, and the fact that I can't make out ANY shapes or hues or variations, I'm honestly concerned that I might be blind for life. What am I going to do for the rest of my life? I can't be blind filmmaker! I'd end up with practical jokers for Cinematographers who'd make sure the film was pointed at the floor the whole time, and assuring me it's the greatest footage ever filmed. I could still write, sure, but I'd have to hire someone to actually type stuff for me. Imagine if I wrote an entire novel or screenplay with my fingers one key over from the home row. Almost everything I enjoy in life involves SIGHT, and now I may have lost it for good. This is so much worse than not having socks.

I don't have time to deal with that fear though, because this entire situation with driving has completely flipped Gertrude out. So I'm trying to calm her down, which means staying calm myself. We sit in the car with her sobbing, and me trying desperately to make out ANY sign of my vision returning. Gertrude had many great qualities, but I'm still amazed how in this situation she didn't even once seem to think about me or my fears. Still, keeping her calm kept me calm, so if we wanted to pretend we could claim that she was actually pretending to be freaked out because it was the only way to keep me calm. Truly she was just being self-centered.

After about 15 minutes my vision began to come back, and once I could see again, Gertrude calmed down and went back to sleep. Why shouldn't she? She'd just been through a horrible traumatic event, it must have worn out her already exhausted body. Me? I'd just had a peachy keen time, so it was only natural that I should drive the rest of the way home.

The rest of the drive was uneventful, but it will remain one of the scariest moments of my life.

Superheroes Need Sleep Too

Who creates college class schedules? And which one of them thinks that the best class to have at 8 am is a history class. And not an exciting history class, a history class about...like...boring stuff. If you want to teach me history at 8 am, there better be strippers involved if you want me to even have my eyes open.

Who actually wants to listen to some tenured professor droning on about the Visigoths when all they can think about is that nice comfortable bed they left behind (and potentially the even nicer and more comfortable girl who's still in it, sleeping away.) Although history classes aren't the worst thing to have first thing in the morning, film history classes are.

Most film analysis classes follow the same pattern, one or two days of lecturing (depending on the schedule) and one day of watching a film to be discussed the next week. And I've seen some interesting films in these classes. One situation I hope to never relive is when we watched

The Dreamers, which features a very attractive French girl, naked, A LOT. Eva Green, if you're reading this, you're absolutely stunning, and I'm incredibly single. Sitting in a room full of people whilst being intensely aroused is a very uncomfortable feeling, only mollified by the fact that every other person in there with a Y chromosome was probably going through the same thing (and probably a few of the double X chromosomes too, this was college).

But you don't watch The Dreamers at 8am in film history. No, you watch Fall of the House of Usher, or Nosferatu. You watch black and white silent films. The problem here isn't so much the black and white (because there are some incredible black and white films out there that I'd put up against anything Hollywood can put out today), it's the silent part. Silent films make me a little sleepy under the best of circumstances; 8 am is NOT the best of circumstances. Early Film History is the only film class I ever failed and had to retake, and when I retook it, I slept through all the films again. Luckily the tests didn't change from one time to the next, so I'd memorized enough answers to get by.

I swear I've still never seen a single frame of The Fall Of The House of Usher (which apparently isn't about a movie theater employee or a rapper) or Nosferatu, but I was in a room while they played, twice.

But I'm not here to talk to you about Film History, no, that's far too interesting for 8 am. I'm here to talk to you about regular good old fashioned History. I'll at least give this particular history professor credit, he tried to make things interesting the first day. The first day of any class is almost universal, the professor gives you a syllabus, explains his absentee policy (and I always kept track of how many classes I could miss how many times, man I loved college), and they give you the same speech about how they hate seeing cell phones in their classroom. To be fair, I don't blame them, if I was trying to teach a class I'd get royally pissed if I saw students busy texting or whatever. It'd almost anger me as much as seeing cell phones in a movie theater, but I digress. He explained to all of us his cell phone policy in his class, he would only allow us to have a cell phone in class under one of two circumstances. The first is that the president's life was in our hands. The second is that we were Superman. But he said that if we were Superman, we'd have to prove it by ripping open our shirt to reveal the costume.

Now would be a good time to tell you about the trunk of my car. I have no idea how it started, but one day it was apparently decided that my trunk would become the repository of all things that might ever be useful under any possible circumstances, as well as things that would never be useful under any circumstances. I'd list for you some of the things in my trunk, but you honestly wouldn't believe me. In fact I'd swear that some of the things in my trunk were never actually put in there. I'm starting to think that the oddities contained in my car are somehow breeding, and giving birth to little monstrosities when I'm not looking. However, the number of times I've been in a circumstance where I was able to solve a problem by saying "I've got one of those in my trunk" would blow your mind. I bring all of this up, because I did in fact have a Superman costume in my trunk. A nice expensive Superman costume, with fake muscles and everything. I fit those muscles like they were a Jell-O mold. Seriously, if I took it off fast enough, you could still see where they were.

So the next day of class I'm sitting in the back of the room, wearing a Superman costume underneath a large black trench coat. Daniel calls my cell phone at the prearranged time, and the professor glares at me with hate in his eyes. I answer it; the students are for the very first time in this class fully awake. I say into my cell "I'll be right there!"

The professor demands to know what's going on, and explains that he was very clear about his feelings about cell phones in class. That's when I whipped open my trench coat, proclaimed that the President's life was in my hands, and ran from the room with my cape and trench coat flapping in the breeze.

I immediately went home and went back to sleep.

Nobody ever spoke of the incident again afterwards. I think everyone wrote it off as a mass hallucination.

Now, as an adult, I'd like to apologize to that teacher for being so ridiculously childish while he was attempting to impart important information to me. Teachers are more deserving of respect than anyone, they've all chosen a career that is thankless in wages, thankless from the students they forcibly insert knowledge into, and thankless in some third way that would make this sentence really funny if only I could think of it. On the other hand, he was teaching a History class at 8 am, so he totally deserved what he got.

JEFF HILLARY

My Best Friend's Junk

Ok, this is officially the one story in this collection that my parents do not need to read. I mean it, you'll be sorry. Also any readers who up to this point have really enjoyed how strongly heterosexual I come across may want to skip this one too, we're going to dabble a little in the slightly gayish territory now.

Allow me to introduce you to my best friend Gary. He's a hell of a guy. Honestly, Gary is a much better person than I'll ever be. I've said this many times. I do the right thing when it's not horribly out of my way, or there's a cute girl to impress, I consider myself a decent person. Gary is incapable of not doing the right thing. It doesn't even occur to him as an option. Also, his voice is quite impressive; it was built for voice-overs and radio work. Sadly he's instead going to be a Philosophy professor. This is because he's exactly the kind of guy that being a Philosophy professor appeals to. His only real problem is that he is painfully and absurdly shy. Well ok, that's not his only problem. He's a fairly scrawny guy, and one of the most fragile people I've ever met. I once watched him hurt himself pretty badly by rolling his eyes too hard. A pat on the back is likely to floor the guy.

So with those facts in hand, can someone please explain to me why Gary has the largest penis anywhere outside of professional porn.

I mean seriously? He's scrawny, he's one good sneeze away from being in a coma, and he has NEVER been able to actually talk to a woman in his life. With all that in mind, between his legs he's a freaking donkey. Life is pretty funny sometimes.

"How do you know this to be true?" I can hear you asking me, (I have very acute hearing). The explanation requires the introduction of one more character.

Enter Jennie. Jennie and I had been friends nervously on the cusp of dating for a long time. Tragically it was never meant to be (and that's all I'm saying on that topic, because if I tried to actually tell the story of Jennie and me, they'd reclassify this book as science fiction, or horror). But all that matters for this story is that she was absolutely my perfect look. If I were to order my ideal woman from a Build-A-Babe shop, she would look like Jennie. Long blonde hair, trim physique, nose just big enough to not be non-descript (I like noses with character, sue me.). She was my physical ideal.

At this time Daniel and I are living in a three bedroom apartment with my friend Princess (for the last time, yes I have a friend named Princess, can we quit harping on minor details?). Princess had just broken up with a boyfriend, and she was very upset. She'd cocooned herself in bed, and if you didn't know better you'd swear she had the flu. So Gary and his wife Hillary came over and Jennie was already staying with me.

Yes, despite the description I gave earlier, Gary does have a wife. I'm largely responsible for that fact. Since Gary lacks any self-promotion, I took it upon myself to promote him, and was incredibly successful. Gary and Hillary have been happily married for many years. This is mostly facilitated by the fact that Hillary is as outspoken as Gary is shy, and as social as Gary is…..not…..social. And yes, my best friend's wife has the same first name as my last name. If you think that's something original or new to point out, you've got a long line of people in front of you.

Anyway, we all pile into Princess' room determined to try and make her feel better. After a while Hillary offered to show Gary's penis to Princess to cheer her up. I'd really like to take a moment to enjoy the sheer artistry of that sentence. Hillary, in an attempt to cheer up the sad Princess, offered to show off her husband's junk. See what I meant about her being outspoken and social?

Gary of course objected to this idea. Imagine, someone too modest to whip out their privates on demand….what a shocking world we live in. Now, we'd all heard about Gary's member, and even as straight as I am, I must confess to a certain morbid curiosity. Jennie, in an attempt to sweeten the deal, offered to get completely naked for everyone, if Gary would only unleash the legend. There was not a single person in the room who didn't want to see Jennie naked (even though I already had a couple of times, it was always a sight well worth seeing).

This was enough to convince Gary that it was worth it. First Jennie stripped down for everyone, which was widely enjoyed by all, and then it was Gary's turn. With his wife's help we were all given a view of the mighty Gary Sr. (because if anything, the actual Gary is the smaller one).

Now, some of you might think it gay of me to not turn away, or run from the room, rather than see my best friend's junk. To you I say NAY! There was a very attractive naked blonde in the deal. Plus, considering how it had been built up in song and legend, coupled with the unlikely nature of a man built like Gary to have anything worth singing or legending about, it was almost akin to getting to look at Bigfoot. I was there for SCIENCE!

Rather than get any more graphic and disturbing than this story already is, I believe I will let Princess' words describe the event for you. It is worth remembering that Princess is quite a teeny-tiny little person. Upon witnessing Gary Sr., all Princess had to say was,

"Ouch!"

So, should you ever hear the tales of Gary Sr., be it from a traveling bard, or the big budget Hollywood blockbuster I'm in the process of writing, I'm here today to tell you that the legend is true, so incredibly, terrifyingly true.

God help us all.

Also I feel here might be an appropriate place to share a little side story. Apparently any group of friends that's been together long enough will contain in it's storied past more than enough tales of uncomfortable nudity to make everyone involved a little ashamed. It's with that thought in mind that I will briefly share the tale of when Gary's wife saw me naked.

I'm in the shower at my apartment, doing showery like things. As my shower draws itself to it's inevitable conclusion, there is suddenly a loud POUNDING on the door. I assume Daniel needs to use the bathroom, and since I am at all times a kind and conscientious person, I get out of the shower and inform him that I'll be out in a second. The pounding continues unabated. I hurriedly towel off, informing him again that I need just a second. The pounding continues. I offer one last warning, "If you don't knock that off, I'm opening the door RIGHT NOW! AND I'M NAKED!" This last bit hurled like the direst threat. The pounding continues. Worked up into a fit of rage now, I fling open the door. I make no attempt to hide myself. I am standing not only naked, but possibly posing in such a way to empathize this fact. Basically the effect I'm going for here is "I warned you to knock it off, you chose poorly in refusing. As your punishment, here is my penis."

It was not Daniel on the other side of the door.

It was Hillary.

At this point some very fierce and swift mental calculations had to be done. The first thought was that obviously she didn't need to use the restroom, she had done this just to annoy me. The second that was that she had succeeded in her goal. The third thought was that the expected response from me now was to cover up in shame. The fourth thought was that this would give her a second victory. The final thought was that I've never been a person to back down, especially when I'm wrong.

And so, seconds after opening the door naked, face to face with my best friend's wife, my response was to yell "WHAT!?" without changing my body's position in any way. She calmly announced that her and Gary were there to hang out. I responded with an incredibly lame "Ok, I'll be out in a second." She walked away, I got dressed, and then there was hanging out.

To this day she claims to have blocked the vision of me naked from her memory. I think it's because she couldn't stand to be tormented by the images of something she could never have…a wet, naked, angry man.

The Great Platypus Caper

My friend Kyle and I stole a platypus.

Once again, heavily tempted to let that be the entire chapter, because it's all downhill from there.

We're going way back now, earlier than any other story yet told. I'm in high school, and my buddy Daniel has a huge crush on Stacy. As is typical in high school romances, Stacy is hesitant to date Daniel, for whatever reasons. She finally decides to issue him a challenge. If he can bring her a platypus, she'll be his girlfriend (or have sex with him, or maybe just kiss him, I don't remember). Daniel is defeated, for how is a man supposed to get a platypus in Texas? Such a task is clearly beyond mere mortals. It would truly be a task for a God...no, even that is not enough. Such a mighty task would take two Gods. That's when Kyle and Jeff spring to the rescue. I'm always willing to be a bandit for love.

Now, Dallas has a very excellent zoo, which was key to our plans. That was the night Kyle discovered that platypi (a word spell-check was never prepared to encounter) have poisonous claws (my editor has pointed out to me that what they actually have is venomous ankle spurs, clearly a very vital and significant difference, thank you Alice). Did you know that? I didn't know that, but Kyle certainly found out the hard way.

We tossed the platypus into my trunk (where it could happily romp with the old issue of Playboy and the pull down screen for passport photos, amongst many other odd things) and drove out to meet Daniel and Stacy. Upon arrival Daniel removed the platypus from my trunk (being careful of the claws, as we'd learned to be) and handed it over to Stacy. Stacy declared the entire deal null and void, since Kyle and I had retrieved the platypus instead of Daniel. My argument that Daniel retrieved it from my trunk, where it just so happened to be, did not sway her. Daniel got nothing. But Daniel did not give up hope, inspired by the heroic courage, daring do, and general handsomeness of Kyle and myself (or so I like to pretend), Daniel went on to make future attempts to woo the mighty Stacy.

That is how I tell the story in person, and it's a pretty decent story. But I promised that the stories in this book would be completely factual, so I should include the missing information.

The platypus that we captured was in fact one of my sister's Beanie Babies. We did consider stealing one from the zoo, until we learned that they didn't have any platypi (sorry spell check), so that part is true. Kyle did research in an encyclopedia and discover about the claws (and reading is always the hard way for Kyle to learn something), so that part is true. We asked for permission to borrow the platypus, but were firmly denied on the grounds that we couldn't be trusted with a small stuffed toy platypus. This meant we had to steal it, so that part is true.

But see how much better a story can be when you remove certain elements?

Oh, and the platypus was returned unharmed, and my family never knew it was stolen, until now obviously.

That was not Daniel's last attempt to get anything from Stacy. The story that follows is very odd, but I promise it is entirely true. The decisions that feature in this story made sense at the time they were made, even if I can't justify them fully now.

Daniel and I went to Rocky one night, where Stacy was the boss. Now, one of the girls on cast had become creepy and stalkerish towards me, and I feared being alone with her at any point. My personal preference would have been not to go at all, but Daniel asked me to help him out. Little did I know what helping him out would entail.

Now, in order to avoid being somehow trapped alone by my stalker, I arranged to have my friend Ivy come with me, on the condition that she be handcuffed to me the entire time. Like I said, it must have made sense at the time. The part of this I find most confusing is, why the hell did she agree!? Ivy will not feature in any other stories, so there's not much point in you the reader actually getting to know her. But she was far more attractive than any girl I should ever be legally allowed to be handcuffed to.

Nevertheless, the show went well and afterward we were all hanging out in the parking lot, as high school kids love to do. I don't recall how the situation initially arose, but Stacy offered to make out with Daniel, but only if he could complete a great and mighty quest first. Having learned from the Platypus Caper that I would find loop holes in any quest she could assign, she issued the only thing that would guarantee my non-involvement.

In order to make out with Stacy, Daniel would first have to make out with me.

So enamored was Daniel, that he did not hesitate before approaching me. I backed away as best I could, but remember I was hindered. Not only was I handcuffed to Ivy, but I'm fairly certain she wanted to see this happen. As Daniel loomed closer, I fought, I really did. Sadly, I could only fight with one hand, and Daniel had the full complement of limbs.

Still, I valiantly and stalwartly (a word I never dreamed I'd actually get to use, and now that I have I'm going to have to go and look it up to see what it means) beat the beast back. I was victorious; I did not have to make out with a man!

And then Daniel pleaded with me. Realizing that were the tables turned, and all that was standing between me and the girl of my dreams was a brief make-out session with a dude, Daniel would have helped me out, I conceded the contest. The things we do for love and friendship.

The mighty Daniel achieved his quest that night, and was rewarded as he was promised.

The only real upside to this entire caper? I got to spend the rest of our friendship pointing out that he was a lousy kisser.

JEFF HILLARY

Insultingly Accepting

My parents have always been very open-minded people, and it's a value they instilled in me from an early age. That's part of the reason I've never been bigoted towards any group in my life. Except furries...furries are disgusting.

Now, growing up wasn't always easy for me. I always had a hard time fitting in at school. I would demand answers to questions nobody in my grade would ever ask. One particular incident was in the first grade, when I DEMANDED to know the purpose of spending an hour colouring in a picture of a hot air balloon. I seriously wanted to know what impact this was meant to have on my education. I clearly knew how to colour, I knew the names of every colour. I knew what a balloon was. So how was sitting down and colouring one for a while supposed to teach me anything at all?

Now that I'm older, I know about the existence and purpose of busy work. Plus I suppose it's possible my peers enjoyed the activity. Me, I wanted to be doing something substantive. Finally the teacher became so upset with my obstinacy that she threatened to send me to the Principal. I called her bluff and volunteered to go visit the Principal, stating that perhaps the Principal would be able to answer a simple question.

Yeah, fitting in was never really one of my strong points. And it didn't get better as I got older. I've always had a need to understand things. I want to know why I'm doing something. This was a problem in school, and would have gotten me shot by friendly fire in the military. Mind you, it wasn't the only problem I had in school, but it's the only one I feel like sharing with you at the moment.

My parents didn't really understand why I had such a rough time in school. They tried to come up with a reason. In their defense, they wanted there to be a single reason I had problems so that they could fight it, and help me out. The idea finally dawned on them that maybe I was gay. It would explain why I couldn't fit in with my peers, and why I always seemed a little out of place.

So sometime in junior high my parents called me into their bedroom, and we had a nice chat. They explained to me that if I was gay, that was ok. They'd still love me and support me, nothing would change, and I should feel free to tell them. Now, being assumed to be gay is a little insulting for any straight guy, but I knew their hearts were in the right place.

Thank goodness all of this happened before I made out with Daniel and saw Gary's junk, because then I'd have had a lot harder time defending my heterosexuality.

I calmly explained to them that I wasn't gay, and they said that if I decided that I was, I could tell them anytime. We left it at that.

OR SO I THOUGHT!

My parents deny it to this day, but that exact same conversation occurred 4 more times over the next 6 years.

Five times my parents let me know it'd be ok if I was gay. Five times. FIVE! At first it was at least a little endearing, but after five times it began to feel like they really wanted me to be gay. Seriously, I began to feel oddly pressured towards homosexuality by my parents. I'm still the only person I know that has a "coming out as a straight man to my parents" story.

Now, the only thing I can say in their defense is, in college I did join the Gay and Lesbian club at school. My reasons for doing so were fairly simple though. I had dated a girl with a gay brother, and she took me to all of the meetings at her school's organization. After that I dated a bisexual girl, who took me to some of the meetings at HER school. Couple that with the fact that my Imaginary Friend Russ is gay, and I finally decided to just join the one at my school. I wasn't the only straight person there, and they were actually a lot of fun to hang out with. Although I will say this, as a straight guy, the worst place to try and pick up chicks is at the Gay and Lesbian club at your high school or college. Seriously, it's just not worth the frustration.

I was even an officer my last semester there. When I ran for Historian I made a little speech introducing myself. I explained that while I was straight, I didn't choose to be that way. They voted me in unanimously, although the fact that I was running unopposed helped.

And after all of that exposure, and my parents constantly hounding me with "are you gay yet? How about now?" I did honestly consider whether or not I could be gay. I tried to picture in my head what it would be like to be in a relationship with a guy. I suppose I could get used to holding hands, maybe even cuddling....but it all falls apart when I try to picture kissing a guy. I am 100% straight, but at least I gave it a shot.

Anyway, the final time my parents called me into their room for this little chat, I'd really had enough. Also at this time I was in a very serious relationship with a girl. In fact I was missing quite a bit of class because we were spending so much time in bed.

Finally fed up with this line of questioning, I did what I think very few men have EVER done in their lives. I offered to bring my girlfriend over and allow them to watch us have sex.

Yes it was awkward. No they did not take me up on that offer. But they never brought up the subject ever again.

In retrospect, I suppose I could have just let them look at some of the porn on my computer. Still, it worked. My sexuality has never since been questioned...by my parents.

Almost Hollywood

As I may have hinted at in previous stories, I've spent the last couple years working in the film industry. The experiences I've had and the lessons I've learned are enough to fill a book (and maybe someday they will). However, I'm assuming most of you have never worked on a film set before, and with that in mind, I'd like to give you a small sample of why movies are so expensive.

This particular story takes place when I was working on a film that will remain unnamed (because I may have to work with some of those people again in the future.) Now, this was a very small production. While I don't know the budget for sure, it was probably around $60,000 or so. Not everyone who was working on the film was getting paid, and the crew that were getting hotel rooms had to sleep up to five people in a room. I elected to sleep in my car. More accurately, I borrowed my parent's SUV with the back seat removed, and using several layers of blankets and pillows I managed to turn it into a small efficiency that I lived in for most of the shoot.

Now that you have a general feeling of the level of production, let's commence with our actual story shall we?

The finale of this movie involved a high school play,

which meant we needed a LOT of extras to be the audience roughly two hundred. These extras joined us around 3pm. They sat down in their seats and were told to keep quiet while everyone worked. Also seated in the audience was going to be the main character's family. The problem with this was that the actress playing the mother did not arrive in town until about 10pm.

After she was done with hair and make-up, we shot the scene somewhere around 1 or 2 am (we shot other scenes that didn't require the extras until then).

If I told this story to someone working in Hollywood, they wouldn't bat an eye. But allow me to point out a few salient details.

First, the extras weren't paid. Put yourself in this mindset. You're going to a little podunk Texas town (and trust me, this town had NOTHING worthwhile in it, I looked) where you are going to sit and do nothing for almost 12 hours. You do this not for money, but for the hope that when the camera briefly pans over a crowd of 200 people, you can point to your face for the .5 seconds it'll be on the screen, and say "THERE I AM!" I've done a few extra gigs in my time, but I've never done them for free. That's just insane. Nine times out of ten you aren't going to ever be seen on camera, and even if you are it doesn't help pad your resume, because any casting director worth his salt ignores extra gigs you've done in the past.

Second, since the extras were there for so long, we had to feed them. Picture in your head the amount of chaos involved in feeding two hundred people in the course of an hour. They all got A sandwich, and even that was tricky to pull off. It also meant that some of the crew had to skip eating that day (or eat with the extras) because it was their job to ensure that these two hundred people all got fed in a relatively orderly manner.

Third, while we weren't paying the extras, we did have to pay for that food. We also had to have crew with the extras at all times to keep an eye on them. Extras can be tricky creatures, and if left alone they can get into all kinds of mischief. You need crew to keep them away from bright lights, prevent them from getting wet, and make sure they don't eat after midnight.

Now there is a clear and obvious alternative to this insanity. Leave a hole where the family will be sitting and film crowd reactions around it. Once that is done you can send home about one hundred and seventy extras. Just keep the ones that will be seated around the family. You then film tighter shots of the family, and cut back and forth between that and the large one. Doing this means only feeding thirty people instead of two hundred people. It also means that those mischievous extras aren't on set any longer than they need to be. They get to go and have lives.

However, since we weren't directly paying the extras, nobody cared how long they waited around. The extras, despite vastly outnumbering the cast and crew, were the least important thing that day.

This is a tiny sample of what makes filmmaking so expensive. Even though I knew how to simplify the process, I was not in a position where anyone would have listened to me. Likely the audacity of voicing such an idea would have gotten me fired from my non-paying gig.

It just seems to me that there has to be a way to balance the Hollywood style of shooting with the common sense required to shoot on a much more limited budget. The biggest issue seems to be that the more people you have working on your crew, the harder it is to let common sense rule the day. The solution to this conundrum? I'm not sure yet, but I'm working on it.

As a brief side note, the day before we used many of the same extras to film a parade sequence. The parade was set during the summer in the film, but was shot in December. Now I realize December in Texas isn't as bad as it would be up north. Since the scene was in the summer, none of the extras (including very little children) were allowed to wear jackets, nor could they even appear to be cold. Making people parade down the street over and over in 20 degree weather, dressed in shorts and t-shirts was kinda fun. I stood there in my jacket, with two shirts on underneath, and wearing two pairs of pants, plus gloves, chuckling all the while.

I really do prefer life behind the camera.

Furry Felines of Furious Fortitude

I'm going to let you in on a secret. Likely after this secret you'll think less of me, but bear in mind I didn't have to share this secret with you.

I'm scared of cats.

No, not like cougars and lions. House cats, the ones we pretend to have domesticated. Now, I don't hate them, but I suffer a literally paralyzing fear of them.

This is the only fear that I have. High spaces, cramped quarters, death, public speaking, these things bother me not at all. Only cats. It is a completely irrational fear, I'm aware. It's irrational for several reasons.

First, I'm pretty sure I could take a cat in a fight. In fact, I would dare say that I could take MANY cats in a fair fight, even more if I was allowed a baseball bat. So why should I fear that which I can overcome with relative ease?

Second, if somehow the cats got the drop on me and

managed to kill me, that's fine. Now, I'm not suicidal, or even depressed, I just suffer no fear of death. All of us are going to die sooner or later. Some of us may live to a ripe old age and pass away in a hospital with machines violating all of our orifices. Others might die peacefully in their sleep (like my uncle). Still others may die screaming in a horrible car wreck (like the passengers in my uncle's car). The fact remains, none of us are getting out of this alive, and we may as well enjoy it. That said, why should I be scared of anything if I'm not scared of the termination of my life?

As a brief aside, I did not have an uncle who fell asleep while driving a car, thus dooming him and his passengers to death. I didn't even come up with the joke in the first place. I apologize for misleading you and promise not to do it again.

Third, I don't fear the big cats (the aforementioned cougars and lions as examples). Now if you locked me in a cage with one, I'd be a little apprehensive perhaps, cautious even, but ultimately I'd prefer it to being in a room with a house cat.

Lastly, I am not scared of kittens. Seriously, itty bitty kittens are adorable. How can you not love them and want to play with them? Now please someone explain to me how my brain decides not to be scared of something until it reaches a certain age, and then it's terrifying?

I don't care if your cat weighs 500 pounds and is essentially a sofa that never moves. I don't care if it's the sweetest, gentlest cat in the world. I don't care if "he's like a dog really". If it's a cat, I fear it deeply. I sometimes have nightmares about a demon cat trying to kill me. I never have anything but pillows to hold it off with. I never win the fight, I just keep trying to hold it off until I wake up.

I can't even say for sure how this fear began. My best guess is when I was attacked by my babysitter's cat at a very young age. He was supposedly the nicest and sweetest cat in the neighborhood, until I went to pet him. Now I swear to you, I did nothing but attempt to pet the cat. I wasn't trying to hit it, taunt it, abuse it, frighten it, molest it, or rape it. I went to pet the cat, and was clawed. Even today I can see the scar (although it's so faint I don't show it to anyone out of embarrassment).

Another source might have been the movie Bedknobs and Broomsticks. I watched it several times as a kid, and just rewatched it as an adult. The cat in that movie is terrifying. I think it's actually the cat that features in my nightmares.

Anyway, this unique fear has caused me to be the subject of scorn and derision on many occasions, as well as putting me in some sticky situations. What follows are a collect of cat stories.

My grandfather had a cat. Nobody liked this cat, but nobody liked my grandfather either, so it worked out pretty well for them. When I would stay at my grandfather's house I would usually sleep on a couch (until my mid 20's, when I argued for a right to sleep in one of the 5 bedrooms). The first night I slept there after he got the cat was one that will live with me forever.

I'm suddenly woken up from my slumber to find the cat laying on my chest staring at me. I can not move. I can't cry out to my sister on the next couch over to help me. I can't roll over to dislodge the cat. I can not move. As I stare at the cat he very slowly and purposefully closes his eyes and goes to sleep. I spend the next 7 hours staring at the cat. After that night my sister often would help me trap the cat in an empty bedroom before we went to sleep. We made sure it had a nice comfy bed, and we always let it out in the morning.

I've NEVER let my fear of cats lead to abusing cats. I have nothing but contempt for anyone who would abuse an animal, especially domesticated ones that have been taught to trust and relay on us. What kind of person can honestly violate that kind of trust?

My friends have always known of my fear, it's impossible to hide. One day I was invited over to a friend's apartment. She realized I was terrified of cats, and she had what seemed to be dozens of them. Commando style she herded the cats to one side of the apartment while escorting me into her room. This is when the problem struck. The doors on either side of her bedroom had been modified so as to allow the cats easy passage from one room to another. These weren't cat-flaps, these were just big squares cut out of the doors. She quickly blocked the squares with plastic tubs. This alerted the cats that something was going down. Suddenly from both sides countless hordes of cats began pawing at the plastic tubs. Plastic SEE-THROUGH tubs. I could WATCH the cats trying to get to me. It was worse than any scene from Aliens, and quite honestly worse than any demon-cat nightmare I've ever had. I honestly don't remember how I got out of that apartment, I think I may have passed out.

My biggest problem with this fear is the paralyzing

factor. When I see a cat, especially if I'm not expecting to see one, every muscle in my body freezes, and I can NOT unfreeze them. The best example is when I left my apartment to go to work one day. I locked the door behind me, turned around, and there was a cat on the other side of the hallway. It stared at me, making it very clear it had no intention of moving. I stood there for 30 minutes. At any point I could have reached my hand back about two inches to knock on my apartment door. Daniel would have answered and rescued me. two inches was way too far for frozen muscles. After 30 minutes Daniel did emerge however, as he had work as well. Upon opening the door and seeing me still standing practically in the door frame, he asked "Where's the cat?" Once he realized I couldn't respond, the lifted me up and moved me out of the way so that he could shoo off the cat. He was my personal hero that day.

One last story, and of a different sort. A homeless cat had taken up residence in our apartment complex. Daniel and his friend David named is Sirius (they were both astronomers, and thought themselves quite clever naming a cat after the "dog-star".) Even I would on occasion leave out food for Sirius, but I'd never go near him. One day when I was going to the gas station Sirius quickly rushed in through my open door and curled up by my back window. I was flabbergasted. Part of me just wanted to lock up the car and run away, possibly to another country. I couldn't do that though, I didn't want to be responsible for the cat's death, nor be without my car until it did pass on. I tried to shoo the cat out of my car, but it was very happy where it was. Finally I performed the bravest act of my life. I got in my car. I think I drove about 10 miles per hour to the gas station, watching the cat in my rear view mirror the entire time. Sirius never stirred. Finally when I got back home, he got out. I decided at that point that I had a pet cat. A pet cat that terrified me, and probably secretly wanted me dead.

Later that winter we had a particularly bad cold snap. The temperature got down to the single digits. I told Daniel that we simple could NOT leave Sirius out in that weather. Daniel was a cat lover, but still wasn't entirely sure about my plan. We had no litter box, and pets were against the apartment code. I finally persuaded him to line the bathroom with newspapers and put the cat in there for the night. True, he'd be locked in a small room all night, but it was going to be better than sleeping in the freezing cold. What happened when I needed to go to the bathroom that night? I didn't, I held it, like a man, a very very scared little man.

I've been working very hard on my fear over the past several years. I've even progressed some. If I know there's going to be a cat, I can move around it....unless it gets close enough to touch me. Even an unexpected cat doesn't cause me to lock up for more than a few minutes anymore.

I think ultimately there is probably a simple way to cure this fear. Since I don't fear kittens, all I need to do is raise a cat from a kitten. Seriously, after caring for a living creature for a year or so, I doubt I'll wake up one day terrified of the thing.

I may even do that someday, but for now I'm sticking with my dog.

Healthy Eating

I'm a bad eater. As a child I was a legendarily picky eater, and as an adult I'm only mildly better. I went through phases in my younger years where I would ONLY eat Cheer-ios, or ONLY eat hot-dogs, but the hot-dogs had to be in a piece of white bread, not a bun. I've never been good at eating vegetables and fruits. I'm not a big fan of my food mixing on my plate. I don't like pizza for this reason.

As I got older I tried to expand my palate. I didn't do this out of a desire to be healthy, but so that getting food for me wasn't such a chore. If someone at work is doing a food run for eight people, you don't want to be the guy who says "grab me a cheese burger, but with no ketchup, no mayo, double down on the mustard, light on the lettuce, and pickles on the side". First of all, you're going to make an enemy of the person getting your food, and secondly they're going to mess it up.

Even now, when I arrive at a restaurant for the first

time I will scrutinize the menu, desperate to find something that I won't have to change into a special order. It's not a matter of being ashamed, or scared of drawing attention to myself. It's much more that I don't want people to make a fuss over me, and the more complicated you make an order, the more likely someone is going to mess it up.

I've gotten to the point where I can eat at almost any kind of restaurant. Most people don't even realize what an incredibly picky eater I am. On rare occasion I'll even try new things. A co-worker from Kenya once brought some grilled goat into the workplace and offered it to everyone. True, it took me days to get the noxious and caustic taste of goat out of my mouth, but I tried it.

Now, all of that said, I grill an amazing steak; you should come over and try it sometime. It only took me 28 years of life to finally convince myself to start eating baked potatoes as well. The final determining factor in the Great Baked Potato decision was that anything containing bacon, cheese, and butter HAD to be good. This is one of my core philosophies of life, as you'll soon see.

But it's because of this culinary limitation that I so love places that thrive on customization of your order. One of my favourite places to eat is a place near my house called Ritzy's. Now, this isn't meant to be an advertisement for the place, but they are incredible. They primarily do burgers, chicken sandwiches, hot dogs, all those things we Americans consider fine cuisine. What they are most famous for though, is their custom salad bar.

They've got every topping imaginable, and a couple I'm scared to ask the identity of. They have four different types of lettuce, and dozens of dressings. You can add in strips of chicken, prepared three different ways. Also, the salad bowls are literally the size of your head. I can only ever eat a Ritzy's salad if I'm starving before I get there. After eating a Ritzy's salad, I have no need to eat for the rest of the day. This is no exaggeration. I had one today at 1pm, and as I write this it is 2am, and I haven't eaten anything since, nor am I hungry.

Now these amazing salads don't come cheap. With a drink, and adding some grilled chicken, they usually come to about $10. However, the owner knows me by now. He seems to think that my name is "Hey film guy, when you gonna put me in your next movie?" (which is a really long and cumbersome name), but he gives me half off everything I order, so he can call me anything he wants. I love this place.

Considering what I've told you about my intensely picky habits, you're probably wondering what sort of things I get on my fabulous salad. By the way, I'd like to point out that fabulous was your word, not mine, but whatever, I don't judge.

I warn you now: my salad is not for the faint of heart, nor for the slim of waistline. My salad is exactly the same every time I go there, half the time I don't even have to tell them the ingredients anymore, they just make it for me. I start out with iceberg lettuce, since it is the least nutritional of all the lettuces (it's important to make sure they don't accidently sneak any kind of healthiness or nutrition into my salad). I then have them add a few onions, just in case any woman was thinking about possibly making out with me (this is a much bigger punch line than you know; trust me, women everywhere are falling out of their chairs laughing at the mere thought of making out with me). Then comes the exciting part, I demand copious quantities of bacon bits and cheddar cheese. Oh yes. I have made them go in the back to find more bacon and cheese to satisfy my cravings. Then I have them add a mountain of croutons, some grilled chicken (the grilled being the healthiest of the chicken, to delude me into thinking that the pile of bacon and cheese won't clog up my heart), and drown the whole concoction in a double serving of honey mustard dressing.

That's right ladies and gentlemen, I, Jeff Hillary, have created the world's unhealthiest salad. I'm tempted to ask them to deep fry it and serve it at the state fair. For those of you who've never been to the Texas State Fair, the food from this past year included chicken fried bacon, deep fried beer, and deep fried lard.

Now, I'm ashamed to admit this, but I don't always manage to finish my meat salad, complete with fresh-made roll. In fact more often than not, I end up leaving half of it behind (these things are HUGE). But on those rare days that I complete the Herculean task of eating a salad I begin to eye the fresh homemade ice cream counter. On those days I know I will be partaking of some chocolate with chocolate chips...yes, I consider every day a war on my body.

The Tale of Jamie

This is one of those times I should really consider changing people's names. Not to protect the innocent, but to protect me from them once they read this.

The tale of Jamie began with Facebook, which is always a dangerous way for something to start. Using this marvel of modern time-wasting, I had decided to reconnect with someone from my past. This particular someone is a young lady named Cynthia, known for her bright eyes, big breasts, and quick sense of humour. I haven't seen Cynthia since my Rocky days, and those were almost 10 years ago.

It turned out Cynthia is an actress these days, and she invited me to come see her latest show. After the show I was invited to hang out with her and some various other people. Now, it becomes clear to me very quickly that I haven't got a chance with Cynthia at all, which is fine (not having a chance with someone is a comfortable feeling at this point, like a nice warm blanket). However, I end up sitting next to Cynthia's best friend Jamie.

Jamie had my complete attention. I don't know if I could exactly point out why. There's really no aspect of her that stands out and demands to be noticed. I remember I liked her hair, and I liked the way she spoke. I also remember her wearing a very unfortunate orange knit cap (which I was later told is yellow, but as I guy I should get credit for remembering ANYTHING she was wearing the first time I met her, seriously). Still, I can overlook that sort of thing in the name of love. It should also be pointed out that Jamie had a really nice butt. I'm not really a butt man, but it did stand out when compared to the fact that her friend Cynthia somehow failed to have any butt at all. I'm still not sure how her pants stay on.

I begin regularly attending Cynthia's performances, always in the hope of running into Jamie again. Sometimes it happened, sometimes it didn't. Any idea of forming a friendship with Cynthia was long gone from my mind. I was focused on her friend, and that was all that mattered.

It was around this time that I began shooting my first feature film. Since Jamie was an actor I asked her to come out and audition. After all, what better way for her to fall madly in love with me than casting her in a film? Yes, I'm an idiot when it comes to women. This will become even more apparent as this story continues to unravel.

Jamie is actually quite a good actress (as well as dancer and singer) and she deserved the part she got in my film. Now I had a problem though. I couldn't ask Jamie out while we were in production. She seemed like she had standards, and when she turned me down it would make the production very awkward. So I put any such plans on the back burner for a while.

Now, during the course of production we did go out to eat one day. I happened to be in the town she lived, so we went and grabbed some cheeseburgers at a bar I knew (I don't actually drink, but I love a good cheeseburger). I didn't really think anything of this; I had done the exact same thing at the exact same place with another actress earlier that week. I did want to try and lay a little ground work with Jamie though.

At a certain point in the conversation I began talking about how I'd been single for quite some time. I explained how I was pretty stupid at understanding women. I told her that the next relationship I was in would probably require the woman to just smack me in the back of the head and say "ask me out, moron." Now, clearly I didn't expect her to reach over at that moment and smack me in the head, but it would have been nice. What a great story it would have been to tell our children. "When your mommy hit me in the head, I knew it was love." Our meal ended, and we return to our normal lives.

True, I didn't call her afterward, but I was terribly busy working on the film, and easily lost track of days. She called me a couple days later, but there was a problem. I was spending time with my Imaginary Friend Russ. Now, I hadn't seen Russ for about a year, and I didn't see him for about 8 months after that. Additionally, I HATE talking on the phone when I'm spending time with someone, it just strikes me as incredibly rude. That, coupled with me being an idiot when it comes to women, caused me to be somewhat more curt than I would have liked, and I ended the call fairly awkwardly.

We fast forward now to the end of production. We are officially done shooting the film, and Jamie

has a brand new play opening up. This is my moment, this is my chance. I buy her a bouquet of flowers (as you should do for any actress you go to see, it's only polite) and steel myself to ask her out after the show.

The show ends (Jamie was excellent, as always) and Jamie and I are talking to each other by her car. It is this moment that she chooses to break up with me.

My brain reeled. She actually told me that she didn't think we should see each other anymore. I wanted to start yelling "WHEN DID WE SEE EACH OTHER!?" but I kept my cool. I tried to explain that I was a confused, but I was actually too confused to explain how confused I was. After she asked if we could still be friends, I realized that this would be a bad time to ask her out.

Driving home that night I began calling friends. I'd just been dumped by someone I didn't know I was dating, and that sort of thing calls for a support network. It is, to date, the absolute lowest point of my entire dating career. I'm hoping it maintains that role for quite some time, because it's hard to think of anything worse (that doesn't involve some kind of severe and embarrassing bodily harm).

It wasn't until later that week I started piecing things together. It turns out she considered our lunch to be a date, which in turn made me a gigantic jerk. I never called her afterward, I never took her out again, and I was pretty short with her when she called me. I suddenly felt like a very horrible person.

Fast forward about a week. I'm at another play, watching another one of my actors. I was actually running late for the play, because I couldn't find the theater. Now, I'm never late. I'm pretty famous for being annoyingly early. Flustered and upset, I run into the theater and grab the first available seat. I turn to my right, and there's Jamie, with her new boyfriend.

The worst part of this entire story? The new boyfriend was uglier than me. That means I ACTUALLY HAD A CHANCE!

Still, it's not a complete loss, because now I get to tell the story of how I was dumped by a girl I wasn't even dating.

Hooray.

The Magical Masturbating Mexican Man

I would like to share a couple of warnings before I start this story. First, it is completely true. Second, the masturbating Mexican man in question was probably not magical in any way. Third, I am not a racist.

Now I know claiming not to be racist is something you do right before being incredibly racist. Normally I would insert here the ethnicities of various friends and/or family members in an attempt to bolster my claim of not being a racist, but using the race of my friends to prove I don't think about race seems self-defeating, and stupid. You will simple have to trust me on this (and after all I've shared with you, why shouldn't you?) when I say that I am not in any way a racist.

I want to make it very, very clear that this story is not meant to be a statement about Mexicans in general. Nor is it a statement about men, masturbation, or magic in general. This story is factual account of a single Mexican man who masturbated, and was only proclaimed to be magical in an attempt to extend the alliteration.

I think this story works best as a cautionary tale. It is very important to check out the area before moving into your first apartment. Ideally you should actually talk to someone that lives in the complex, ask them if there is anything you need to know about it. Offer them money if you have to. Otherwise this could happen to you:

When Daniel and I (and Stacy, but she's not in this story) moved into our first apartment, we lived next door to eight Mexican men. This is a little impressive considering they were living in a two bedroom apartment. The logistics of this arrangement gave Daniel and me hours of contemplative entertainment.

Now, when you have so many people living in such close proximity, I'm assuming that personal space is at a premium. It is this assumption that forms the only possible explanation for what follows.

After living in the apartment for a couple weeks, I learned a disturbing fact. Sometimes when I came home from work, one of the Mexican men would be standing at the top of the stairs talking on the phone, with his hand in his pants. He would see me get out of my car and he'd hang up the phone, remove his hand, and go back to his apartment.

It didn't happen every night, but about twice a week this would occur. Daniel told me he encountered the same thing. Our natural assumption was that he was...manipulating himself. Either he was having phone sex with a girlfriend or it was some kind of sex chat line.

Now, I have no problem with masturbation. In fact,

it's been proven that…releasing…once a day heavily prevents prostate cancer later in life. Now, that release can be achieved with the aid of a partner, but she's not always going to be in the mood. Also, saying "honey, we can just do it quick and get it over with, it's for my health after all" is NOT considered to be romantic, and will likely insure that the only release you find for the next couple of weeks is when you are by yourself. Women are often selfish that way, demanding that they be treated as human beings with feelings and emotions in exchange for the most personal and intimate of acts with them. Prudes.

I am forced to assume that finding the personal time and space to achieve…release…must be tricky when you are sharing one bathroom with seven other men. Also, I'd like to briefly pause to think about the state of that bathroom. Men are fairly disgusting creatures, and eight men in one bathroom? The mind reels from the possibility of envisioning what that must have been like.

The most disturbing part of this ordeal was yet to come though. As the months went by, the man became much less shy about his activity. Rather than stopping when he saw me get out of the car, he'd continue as if nothing was happening. I'd climb the stairs to my apartment, he'd step out of my way, all the while with his hand down his pants. Also, as if this situation wasn't creepy enough, I never heard him say a single word to whoever was on the other end of the phone. For all I know he was touching himself while listening to the Movie Phone guy. It got worse when he would begin to nod at me in greeting as I walked by. It was almost as if he was saying, "Nice night to stand outside and masturbate in front of your neighbors isn't it?"

For the record, it is NEVER a nice night to stand outside and masturbate in front of your neighbors. Not if you're a guy at least. If you're a woman, there's a little room for negotiation.

Once again, I conferred with Daniel, who had the exact same experience (as did Stacy, but she's not in this story). The whole thing was disturbing on a level we'd never experienced before. We knew we were in a rougher part of town. Stacy (who isn't in this story) almost got picked up as a hooker after all. Plus anytime I went walking at night I was offered any drug I could desire. There were even rumours of some axe wielding maniac menacing children with an axe, but that just sounded too absurd to be true.

There isn't a really good resolve to this story. One day the Mexicans moved out, and an astronomy student moved in. To my relief, I never once witnessed him playing with himself.

I often wonder what happened to the Magical Masturbating Mexican Man. My best guess is he was picked up for public lewdness while listening to hold music. He's probably a registered sex offender now. At least I hope so; we can't keep letting these telephiles ruin our society.

Farts Are Funny

This is definitely a story just for the fellas. This story involves flatulence, and a bit of vomit. Seriously ladies, just skip ahead to the next story, this one will only serve to disgust you, and possible switch you to lesbianism.

Before I dive right in to my fantastically funny flatulence fables, I would like to share a word of warning with all of you.

Never fart in a sensory deprivation tank.

I know often when you are given a warning like that; it is incredibly tempting to test it for yourself to see what the person trying to warn you is talking about. This is not one of those situations. There is no need to repeat my mistakes, I suffered so that you wouldn't have to. I almost asphyxiated for your sins. Don't let my suffering have been in vain.

For those that don't know, a sensory deprivation tank is a neat little thing. It's essentially the size of a double large bathtub filled up with heavily salted water. The tub is then enclosed in an air and light tight dome. The water is kept at body temperature, and you wear ear plugs. The outcome of this arrangement is that you can't hear anything, you can't see anything, and after a few seconds floating in the water you can't feel anything (including the water you're floating in). It's an interesting experience, and well worth trying once.

But I made a nearly fatal mistake. After nearly an hour of floating in this water, attempting to achieve some sort of deep cosmic connection to the universe, I felt gassy. Since I'm alone in this tank, I decided to let it go. That's when my sense of smell was awoken with a VENGENCE UNHOLY! The stench was beyond any reason. It was Lovecraftian in its unfathomable malevolence. I only had one sense working, and now it was working overtime. The stench was so abominable that I was forced to vacate the tank prematurely, it was me or the fart…and the fart won. I still sometimes fear my flatulence may have actually gained sentience, and may be hunting me down.

If you take one thing away from this book, just one thing, let it be this: never fart in a sensory deprivation tank.

Now, to the previously promised fantastically funny flatulence fables (for fellas, first and foremost).

I'm always been a pretty gassy guy. My sister Amber has always had a pretty weak stomach. These two events come together like chocolate and peanut butter. They have come together on four occasions, all of which I will recount for you now.

The first time was nothing special, and we were both quite young. For some reason or another I was sleeping on a couch in our house, and my sister on the floor nearby. More than likely I had just told her some scary story or another, and she insisted we sleep in the same room. Right before she drifted off to sleep, I felt some gas building up. I did what any young boy would have done. I sagged my butt off the couch, aimed it at her, and let loose. The reaction was immediate and spectacular. My sister threw up on her sleeping bag. That's when I realized how much fun having a little sister could be.

The second time might actually be my favourite. It was a Saturday, and I was barely a teenager. This meant I didn't have school or a job, and could sleep in as late as I wanted. This particular Saturday I woke up and decided to just stay in bed for a while. It is worth noting at this point that my sister's room and mine were right next to each other. They shared a wall, but it was a fairly substantial one. Suddenly I realized I needed to fart, and it felt like a good 'un. Guys, let me tell you, never before or since have I EVER had a fart like this one. It was as if a solid wall of air emerged from me. The sheets moved, I swear they did. The sheer intensity of volume and air surprised even me. In the next room my sister's dog started barking. I chuckled to myself, and rolled over to return to sleep.

Suddenly my door was flung open and my sister flew in demanding "WHAT THE HELL WAS..." Sadly she never got to finish that sentence. Holding her hands to her mouth and retching, she ran for the bathroom, a mere 4-feet away, and she almost made it before she threw up. It was on that day I decided I was a man.

The third time was perhaps the most crass and gross of all of them, and at that point that's really saying something. My family was driving to Colorado to spend Christmas with my grandparents. It's a 14 hour drive, and I was feeling gassy. As an added bonus, I had my girlfriend with us. I was supposed to bring my previous girlfriend on the trip, but we'd broken up a couple months before, so this girl and I hadn't been dating long at all.

My sister was sitting in the passenger seat of the SUV, and I was in the back seat. Once again I felt that old familiar feeling. This time however, I decided to be diabolical. I stood up and somehow managed to hang my butt next to my sister's head. I then called out her name, and waited what I thought was the right amount of time before I let loose. As my sister scrambled to roll down the window and puke out the side of the vehicle, my girlfriend SWORE that Amber's hair had actually been blown back by the wind. That's when I knew we were in love, until I broke up with her four months later.

Sadly the last time wasn't really particularly notable. It was another Christmas in Colorado. I had just walked into the Den with the Christmas tree and the gigantic pile of presents. As I'd walked in I let loose a little poot. Nothing of any consequence, certainly not one I was proud of. It was so small and insignificant I probably would have blamed it on the cat out of shame. Little did I know my sister was about to walk into the room too. She walked in the doorway, looked at me, and said "Jeff, did you just..." and was again cut short.

She actually threw up into her hands as she fled the room. As she continued to run to the bathroom everyone in the house could hear her resounding cry, "Did I get any on the presents!?"

Man, all these memories of such good times. If you'll excuse me, I think it's time to go visit my sister.

Narrow Escapes

Yes, the stories you've heard are true. I did live in a girls' dorm in Florida for a week. I'm not sure how you found out about it, but I might as well give you the details.

I believe I was a sophomore in college at the time, and over the summer I had dated a girl who had just graduated from high school. Her name was Myrtle. Ok, it wasn't really, but we're doing that whole old lady name instead of ex-girlfriend name, remember? Now, Myrtle was going away to Florida for college, and we both knew it, so we tried our best not to get too attached to each other that summer. Young love doesn't work that way though, you put an obstacle in front of it, and it just GROWS. So when it came time for her to head off to school, we were absolutely smitten with each other.

We saw very little of each other obviously, but we did the best we could. When my spring break came a week before hers, I decided it was time to visit. At that point in my life (like every point before it an since) I didn't have much money, so a hotel was out of the question, nor did I have the money to rent a car. Normally I would have crashed in her dorm room, but she lived in an all-girls' dorm, and boys weren't allowed past a certain time. Sounds like a recipe for adventure!

She lived on the second floor of the building, and her RA (who was always on the lookout for boys where boys weren't meant to be) was in the next room over. If I got caught at any time during that week, I could actually be charged with criminal trespassing. The worst part of the ordeal was that they had community bathrooms, which meant NO BOYS ALLOWED. The only bathroom boys were allowed to use was a half torn up bathroom on the first floor. Luckily this bathroom had a shower...sort of.

What it actually had was something that at some point in the distant past used to be a shower. There was no shower head and almost no water pressure. Also the heater had been removed. What happened when you turned it on was a tiny trickle of freezing cold water would emerge. This was how I kept myself clean for a week.

In order to fully understand the magnitude of misery we're talking here, it's now important to share with you my shower habits. I love hot showers. I tell that to girls, and they always say "me too" and then when I'm showering with them they freak out at how hot it is. To be very clear, my skin is red and the bathroom is so filled with steam that you can't see your way out of the shower. My parents actually had to replace my bathroom wallpaper with just regular paint because I peeled it off with all the steam. Scorching is the word we're looking at here. To go from that on a daily basis to a dribble of water that had NO heat in it at all was an endurance trial. It's the sort of thing Klingons would do to their kid when he becomes a man. It was horrifying, and I did it in the name of love.

Also, as boys weren't allowed in the dorm after 9pm, Myrtle would take me on my last trip to the bathroom (no unescorted boys at any time) around 8. If I needed to pee between that and 11 o'clock the next morning, (when boys were allowed in again) that was just too bad.

One particularly notable incident was when the RA began to become suspicious that my girlfriend had a boy over, and came to investigate. Luckily my girlfriend's room had a window in it that led to a portion of the roof. So there I am on the second story roof, wondering if I'm going to have to try and jump off to avoid jail time, and I can't help but feel that this was all so familiar.

You see, the year before I'd been dating another girl. Remember Gertrude from the night I went blind? Yeah, she lived in an all-girl dorm at a college within driving distance of me. I frequently spent the night there illegally. At least Gertrude's room had a sink in it, which she allowed me to pee in. However, one day there was rumours of a boy in the dorm, and the RA was on a rampage. I hid in closets, I was shuffled from room to room, but there was just no way to get me out of the building unseen. The worst part was I needed to get to work, and time was running out. Finally, I decided to do something very stupid (which is really not unusual for me), I was going to leap out of the second story window to escape and go to work.

Now, nature was in my favour, it had actually rained a lot the night before and the ground was nice and muddy (messy, but soft). I handed Gertrude my new expensive trench coat, and told her to throw it out to me after I landed, so I wouldn't get it muddy. She begged me not to jump, but I was far too male for common sense. I leapt out of the window, and just barely avoided hurting myself landing. As I shakily stood up and turned I saw my trench coat hit me in the fact and knock me down again (it's a heavy coat and I was poorly balanced, shut up). Gertrude had already shut the window. I found out later that the RA had entered the room seconds after I'd jumped out, my timing couldn't have been better.

Luckily, in the case of Myrtle, no such leap was needed. But seriously, ice cold showers and full bladders for a week? Is anything really worth that amount of inconvenience?

Yes, young love.

Tight Spaces

I suck at sleeping. Seriously. There is no part of it that I'm good at. I have a hard time falling asleep under perfect circumstances. Even on days when I'm beyond exhausted, and all I want in the world is sleep, it still takes me at least an hour of tossing and turning to actually fall asleep. I wake up if a fly farts in Africa, or if something thinks my name really hard. It is not uncommon for me to wake up three or four times in the middle of the night. In the morning, I never want to wake up. Unless I have an actual commitment that requires me to be somewhere at a certain time, dragging myself out of bed is one of the hardest things I have to do. I'll get in arguments with myself about how much longer I can lay in bed. Sometimes these arguments escalate into physical violence. I may have even called the cops on myself once, but I took me back, because I love me. I don't know if I've ever really been well-rested. This fact has led to the occasional adventure though.

I wasn't sleeping well at home, I don't remember

why. Maybe there was construction, maybe my chi was off, I have no clue. About once a year I get in a mode where my brain goes a hundred miles an hour every night for a week, and sleep is an impossible thing. Or maybe there was a family of crickets living outside my window. It could have been any number of things really. All I remember is it'd been a week since I'd had more than a couple hours of sleep, and I was desperate. Luckily my friend Gary offered to let me sleep on his couch.

Eager for the opportunity to actually sleep, I drove 45 minutes to his place, only to find that he was at work. He was going to be at work for the next four hours. Well I couldn't take any of this awake nonsense anymore and decided to try sleeping in my car. Sleeping in my car is never easy, I'm too big to curl up in the back seat, and the front seat doesn't really let you sleep on your side. When I sleep in my car for film work, it's actually my parent's Expedition that I borrow and fill the back with tons of blankets and pillows.

The last thing I remember is trying desperately to get comfortable enough to pass out for a couple hours until Gary arrives to let me in.

The next thing I remember is waking up somewhere pitch black and very small. I have a decent amount of room around me, but the roof is only inches above me, and I can't see anything. Also I feel that the space is full of....things. I feel something cloth-like, and there are a couple books. When I felt the rubber duckie and the baseball bat, I knew where I had to be. I was in my trunk. It even seems I was using the cape of the Superman costume as a blanket.

I had no memory of getting in my trunk. If you'd asked me before that day I would have sworn I couldn't fit comfortably in it. Surprisingly, it was actually pretty cozy. I fished out my cell phone and used it as a light to look around, and tried to figure out how I'd extract myself. This was not a situation I ever envisioned myself in, but I was trying to be a good sport about it. At least I don't have a fear of enclosed spaces.

It was at this time that I saw a most remarkable thing. Now I don't know if every car comes with this, because I don't really spend a lot of time in trunks, but there was a little lever. There were no words on or around the lever, but there was a picture to describe its function.

The picture was of a little car with an open trunk and a stick figure. Between the car and the stick figure was a dashed line which seemed to imply that the figure had emerged from the trunk and bounced on the ground a couple of times until he was free. The stick figure was smiling though, so I guess the bouncing didn't hurt that much.

The obvious assumption is that the lever was a trunk release in case you were ever taken hostage and shoved in a trunk. To the best of my knowledge I'd gotten into the trunk voluntarily, but I was sure the manufacturers wouldn't mind if I used it.

As the trunk opened, and I emerged into what little daylight was left, I heard a couple of very surprised exclamations. Two people had been standing nearby in the parking lot talking, only to watch me emerge from my own trunk. They looked quite surprised. I waved at them, but they weren't feeling very friendly and just walked away.

Now, you'd think that maybe they put me in the trunk. But you'd be wrong, and should be ashamed of blaming those innocent young people of such mischievous misdoings. It turns out, while I was getting into my trunk, I actually called Gary (and several other people) and explained to them I was getting into my trunk to go to sleep and if I came up as a missing person, that's where I was.

Pretty good proof of my exhaustion right? Not only did I climb into my trunk, but I made multiple phone calls, and didn't remember any of it.

I did sleep in my trunk a couple times after that, since it was so comfy. But I don't do it very often, the weather needs to be just right for it to work, and it gets hot in Texas.

If my car ever gets stolen, I hope it's while I'm fast asleep in the trunk, I'd imagine that'd end up pretty funny, or with me murdered and left by the side of the road.

The Long Imagination of the Law

You know what I haven't done in a while? I haven't shared a story involving socks. Because when you get right down to it, my entire life has revolved around socks to one degree or another.

This one also involves my friend Kyle. You may remember Kyle from the Great Platypus Caper. Kyle and I went on many grand adventures together, sadly most of them weren't real. Rather than tell you about the time he and I sunk Atlantis (which was totally Kyle's fault) or how we sunk the Titanic (more my fault) I'll share a story that actually happened.

We were both in high school at the time, which isn't horribly relevant, but I think it helps you to appreciate the mindset we were in (young and male, which scientifically equals stupid).

Somehow, someway, we had done something to upset Kyle's mother. At this point I can't possibly begin to remember what it was, perhaps she heard about that incident with the Trojan horse. Anyway, it was clear to me that if our fictional adventures were to continue unhindered, we'd need to cheer his mother, and fast.

I suggested we get her a present, and not just any present, but the ultimate present to help cheer up a brooding mother, socks. Even way back then, before either of the legendary sock stories, I knew that socks were of vital importance. What could cheer her up more than a nice, new, comfy pair of socks?

Donning my faithful trench coat (which is showing up in more of these stories than I would have imagined) Kyle and I were off to the Wal-Mart. After perusing the sock selection for far longer than sanity would properly dictate, we purchased the perfect pair of socks.

Now, in our mad fever to bequeath these socks unto Kyle's mother, thus lifting her mood and removing Kyle from the doghouse our actions had (undoubtedly deservingly) placed him in, we chose to race each other back to my car.

This was our mistake, and our downfall.

After running full tilt through the parking lot, we arrived at my car, and leapt in as if we were action movie stars. I started up the car and was about to back out of the spot when suddenly a police car blocked me off, lights flashing and siren blaring. Before I could even get out of the vehicle to preemptively surrender, ANOTHER cop car arrived at the scene. The cop, recognizing what a threat two sock purchasing teenagers presented, had called for backup.

The cop questioned us for quite some time. He

wanted to know what we were up to, I told him we were buying socks for Kyle's mother and showed him the receipt. He wanted to know why we were running out of the store, this was harder to explain, but I settled on the fact that we were merely racing, as teenagers do. He very clearly did not believe our story, even with me offering up the socks and receipt to back our claim. Then came the most confusing part of the ordeal, he wanted to know what we'd done with Kyle's trench coat.

See, he'd already examined my trench coat with his flashlight (did I mention it was night? It was night), searching for weapons I suppose. I would like to take this moment to point out that this was before Columbine, so black trench coats did not have the bad reputation that they enjoy today. The cop was quite insistent that when he saw us running from the store, we were both attired in trench coats. The only problem with the cop's story is that Kyle did not own a trench coat, of any kind.

At this point the cop's backup has gotten out of the car and is watching the entire ordeal. I was nervous (as any teenager should be when confronted with the police) but I KNEW I hadn't done anything wrong. I was also very confused at the cop's repeated claims that Kyle had been wearing a trench coat. He repeatedly insisted we produce the coat for him to examine. When we insisted for the fifth time that there wasn't another trench coat, he accused us of lying. When we swore we weren't lying, he accused us of accusing him of lying. I tried to explain that we were merely accusing him of being misinformed. He didn't like that either.

Finally I gave him permission to search my car, which

he and his backup did, meticulously. They could find no second coat, and this enraged the officer. He gave Kyle and me quite the telling off. The only part of this tirade that I can remember to this day is the following quote.

"I don't know what's going on, but I know you guys are up to something, and I'm going to figure it out and I'm going to come and get you."

I told him again exactly what we were up to: we were buying socks for Kyle's mother. This did not settle his mood as I'd hoped, but he was forced to let us go.

I sometimes like to picture this cop, over a decade later, still dedicated to unraveling the mystery of that night. I picture him with a cork board covered with pictures he's secretly taken of Kyle and me going about our lives. I can see him trying to tie our night of sock buying to major tragedies across the world. Occasionally I lay in bed at night wondering if this will be the night he breaks down my door and hauls me in to face justice.

Man, I hope Kyle never buys a trench coat, or else I'm getting taken to jail. I'm just not sure for what.

And by the way, Kyle's mother was so touched by our purchase that she did let Kyle out of the doghouse, and we went on to have many more adventures that didn't actually happen.

All My Ex's Have Left Texas

The title of this piece, apart from being a clever play on a well-known country song, also happens to be entirely true. In my life I've had 4 serious relationships. Yes, I'm aware that's not a lot, but I'm still relatively young, and I've always been a quality over quantity guy anyway. Of these four girls, absolutely NONE of them live in Texas anymore.

It's really like there's some kind of pre-relationship agreement that in the event of a break-up, I get the state and they get the hell out. I'm actually ok with this. I have a great fondness for this state, as well I should being an 11th generation resident.

But this little oddity is not what you're here to read about, you're here to read about break-up stories. I've got 3 of them for you. To protect myself (legally and physically) I am going to change the names of the three girls. I'd also like to point out that I am well aware that there are two sides to every issue, and if any of my ex's want to state their side, they need only write and publish a book about it.

Let's start with Gertrude shall we? And yes, they are all getting horribly ugly old lady names, because I think it's funny.

Gertrude and I dated for two years, and her parents HATED me. They despised the very ground I walked on. This was an unusual problem for me; I'm usually very popular with parents. I don't drink, smoke, do drugs, have tattoos, or have a criminal history (the great Sock-Buying Caper not withstanding). The primary reason her parents hated me was that I was from Texas. For some reason their daughter chose to leave her home state to go to school here, and her bringing back a Texan was apparently inexcusable. Also they really disliked the fact that I didn't drink. Forget that I was underage at the time, they thought that I was a pussy for not drinking. These two had a very odd set of priorities.

Now, Gertrude was my first girlfriend outside of high school, and I had just moved into my first apartment. I was 18 years old, had a place of my own, and a steady girlfriend. Can you guess where this is going? Gertrude and I discovered that spending time with each other (sometimes even out of bed) was much more fun going to class. Her grades went in the toilet and I flunked out of college altogether (I later went back and excelled, a story for another time). So I don't blame her parents for their next course of action, not really.

Gertrude's parents refused to pay for school for their daughter unless she returned home to do it. Perhaps if they didn't already hate me, we would have just gotten lectured, but the fix was in, and Gertrude was out of Texas.

We tried to maintain the relationship, because we'd been together for 18 months, but it just wasn't working out for me, I couldn't STAND not having her nearby. So I knew I needed to end it. How to end it though? Touchy subject. She frequently would regale me with a tale of one of her friend's long distance relationships. Apparently she went to visit the guy one week, and after the visit was over he called her and told her it was over. Gertrude found this to be abhorrent. So I realized this had to be handled in person.

About that time Gertrude surprised me with a visit to Texas. The entire time she was here I debated with myself whether or not to end it. It was a rough decision. Ultimately, the night before she was due to fly back home, I broke the news to her. She collapsed to the ground wailing and ripping up grass. She kept yelling "this isn't happening, this is a bad dream, and when I wake up I'm going to kill myself." So she took it exactly as well as I'd expected.

It was a long and uncomfortable night, but that was only the beginning. The next morning I drove her to the airport. It's about a 30 minute drive, and it lasted for WEEKS. My first move was to turn on the radio, which she promptly turned off. So we drove in silence the whole time. At no point in this process did I get points for doing it in person, instead of over the phone, which would have been so much easier.

It was after she left that things got weird. She still called to talk, and I did miss her, and so I kept talking to her. That wasn't fair to either one of us. She said that she would move back to Texas in about a year, and I told her I wouldn't mind us trying again if that happened. Then she went completely off the rails.

She contacted my friend Alice, who I've been friends with since Kindergarten, and told her that I was horribly depressed over this break-up. Gertrude also told Alice that she'd been talking to my mother about how depressed I was, and how we'd be getting back together soon. Alice called me up and tore me a new asshole.

After checking with my mother, who confirmed that there had been NO communication with Gertrude since we broke up, I set Alice straight, and realized that I really only had one option. I stopped taking Gertrude's calls. It was hard, and I felt horrible, I still loved the girl after all. It worked though; she got so angry at me that she was finally over me.

She never did come back to Texas, instead she married a boy from her home state, much to the joy of her parents I'm sure. And if you think I handled that break-up poorly, we're just getting started.

Let's talk about Agnes. I started dating Agnes about two weeks after Gertrude and I broke up. She was absolutely a rebound relationship, one that I managed to make stretch out over 6 months. 6....long...grueling months. Agnes was pretty stupid, and none of my friends or family particularly cared for her. Mind you, most of them didn't like Gertrude either, but they at least respected that we made each other happy. Agnes was just painful. I started dating her because she wanted to go out with me, and I wasn't used to being alone. This is always a solid foundation for a relationship.

I think one of the most irritating things about her was that she was convinced she was smarter than me. While I'm a fairly bright fellow, I won't hesitate to admit there are people smarter than me, I'm friends with some of them. Her reasoning for WHY she was smarter than me should tell you all you need to know about her. She claimed that she was smarter than me because her father had a PhD and mine didn't. When pressed on this issue, she would claim that since intelligence is purely genetic, and since a PhD could only be gotten by someone overly intelligent, I must be the moron in the relationship.

Let's ignore the fact that she was comparing her biological father to my adopted father for a moment and focus on something you guys may not know. Ability to perform in school is not directly correlated to intelligence, at all. My class Valedictorian in high school (a charming young girl, who I never have had a single negative thing to say about) was even known to admit that I (a C-ish student) was smarter than her. She excelled at studying, and thus got the better grades.

As another fun side-note, my sister had a habit of referring to Agnes as Ms. Piggy, claiming that the two looked far too similar to not share some genetic heritage.

So how did Agnes and I end it you ask? Badly, and again, my fault really.

It was the summer break. Agnes had no school, and she had no job. These are facts that will be crucial in a minute. Now, after years of wondering and searching I had found my biological father. He lived about five hours away, and had invited my girlfriend and me to come and visit for a weekend. This was obviously a big deal to me.

I'd talked to the man a couple of times before this, and spent a little time with him, but this was going to be the big trip where I asked the big questions.

I asked Agnes two weeks ahead of time if she'd please come with me. She refused to commit to an answer. This bothered me for a while, but I tried not to press the issue. Finally, two days before I was to drive down there and stay at his house, she called to tell me she wasn't coming. I informed her that I'd already told Chris (my biological father) that she wasn't coming, since I thought it'd be rude to keep him guessing as to the number of house guests until the day before. Making me wonder if I was going alone or not was pretty rude too, but not the point. At this point she got really angry with me. She even yelled at me that she "was too busy and didn't have time for my little field-trip."

Two points, as previously mentioned she had no job or school, so what she was so busy with I'll never know. Secondly, discovering my heritage, where I come from, what 50% of my genetic makeup is like, is a little field-trip? Even now that makes me a little angry.

But I swear to you I did not hang up on her. Either she hung up on me in her outrage at me assuming she wasn't coming, or the phone just disconnected. But rather than call her back and start yelling at her, I simply texted her. "Well, I don't have time to call you back and break up with you, so this will have to do."

Yes, I broke up through a text message. I am a horrible human being. She never contacted me again, even though about a week later she knew I was going in for knee surgery. I did later send her an email apologizing for the way (but not the fact) that we broke up. I tried to explain why what she'd said made me so angry, and caused me to react the way I did. I apologized not in the hope of reconciliation, but merely to clear my conscience of having broken up with a girl through text message.

She emailed me back and told me the reason our relationship never worked was because I have a poor relationship with my family. The family that took me in so I could quit my job and pursue my dream of film making. My family who has never been anything but supportive of me my entire life, and who I continually thank for that fact. My family who not only understood my need to connect with my biological family, but supported it. Yeah, she was pretty stupid.

Before my knee had even fully healed from the surgery, I started dating Myrtle. We seriously tried not to date, but there was no avoiding it. I should have known there was trouble ahead, but what are you going to do?

Myrtle was bisexual, which isn't an issue for me; I have several friends who are. Myrtle has ended her last two relationships with boys because she was worried that she hadn't dated enough girls, and thus hadn't fully explored who she was as a person. I can grant the concern some validity, but both times she started dating another guy within a couple weeks of dumping the previous. And now she was dating me.

I was very much in love with this girl. Not in a creepy stalkery sort of way, but in a boyfriend who can't think of anyone else sort of way. But still the problems began to brew. It didn't help that she ended up going out of state for school. We both knew there was no way for this relationship to last, but we tried anyway. The last time I flew out there to spend my spring break with her was probably the worst trip of my life. She still had school work, and I tried to be respectful of that, I really did. But she spent almost the entire trip treating me like I was an amazing burden to her, like I was ruining her life by being there. All the while introducing me to these guys she had crushes on.

I came back from that trip very unhappy, but determined not to judge an entire relationship by one week. Maybe she was feeling really stressed about school, who knew? I was willing to make any excuses it would take to stay with her. Besides, a couple months later and it'd be summer, and we could spend three whole months together.

Then one night a week later we were chatting online, and she brought up a subject she'd brought up many times before...she was worried that she'd never know herself as a person if she stayed trapped in a relationship with me, instead of dating a girl like she'd always wanted. After the trip I'd had, and the multiple times we'd had this argument, an argument that ended her last two relationships before me, I ended it. I told her she no longer needed to be worried about me, and she was free to pursue any woman she desired.

Yes, I broke up with a girl through online chat. I mean seriously, aren't we supposed to learn from our mistakes? Every break up just gets worse and worse. I'm seriously concerned that the next time I break up with someone it'll be through a note hand delivered by a bum I paid $5. The note will probably just say "Don't call me, you suck."

I regretted breaking up with Myrtle and tried to get back together with her, but I suppose she did both of us a favour by staying strong and turning me down. The long distance thing would have killed our relationship sooner or later anyway. As a fun little side note though, two weeks later she was dating another guy.

So whoever my next girlfriend is going to be, I'd like to apologize now for the horrible manner in which I will break up with you. It's not you, it's me, apparently I'm an idiot.

Who Are These People?

I'm tired of talking about my failure to be able to break up with someone like a decent human being. Let's instead talk about other people failing to do things. Specifically, let's discuss some of the whack jobs we allow to teach college these days.

I was in college for quite a while, thanks to flunking out and then going back to set things right. And while you may remember the tale of me running from class in a Superman costume, I assure you that the insanity was not all on my side of the lecture hall. I had some professors that defied belief, and I'd like to share a few of those stories with you now.

We'll begin with Introduction to Psychology. It wasn't technically a required class, but it's the one most people took to satisfy that portion of the core curriculum. Since it was such a popular class, it took place in the biggest classroom on campus. It was like attending a rock concert every day. Now, usually the first day of class is spent discussing the general tone and aim of the class, going over the syllabus, and (most importantly) discussing the attendance policy. The attendance policy is the most important part because it lets you know how many days you can skip without consequence, and believe me, I skipped as many classes as I could get away with my first couple semesters.

This particular professor did not get that memo about what to do the first day of class. What follows is to my best recollection a verbatim copy of what that magical professor discussed the first day of class, with at least 100 students in attendance. I will get some salient details wrong, but the general tone and gist will be dead on, I assure you.

"There are two things you're going to need to know to get through this class. First is that I'm a Christian, and the second is that I love the name Aristarchus. See, I was reading the Bible not too long ago, as I do, and I discovered that while Jesus had his disciples, apparently those disciples had groupies of their own. There's one passage that names them, and they have pretty boring names, you know, Marks, Peters, Jameses, that sort of thing. Then I came across Aristarchus. How awesome a name is that!? Aristarchus. It's the greatest name I've ever seen. When I die and go to Heaven, I'm not going to ask to meet Jesus, or God, you have to figure that those guys have a long line of people just waiting to meet them. No! I want to meet Aristarchus, because with a name like that you KNOW the guy has to be rocking out. He is absolutely the rock star of Heaven, how could he not be? His name is Aristarchus!" It continued like this for quite some time.

Why I needed to know that my psychology professor was Christian, I don't know. The class had nothing to do with religion, and religion never came up again after this first day. It's roughly the same as if I made a speech before the screening of my latest movie and said "There's thing you need to know before I begin this movie, I eat meat." Then I showed my movie, which was a sci-fi thriller that had nothing to do with dietary habits of any kind.

Why he needed to spend the first day telling us about some D-List Bible celebrity, I also don't know. What I do know is that the name stuck with me. Everything I've ever written has contained a character, or made reference to a character named Aristarchus Johnson. So, while it was insane, and made me fear for my professor's sanity, he did manage to have a lasting impact on me. And I hope it has an impact on all of you. I think if we all pull together, we can make Aristarchus the #1 baby name in America.

Next we'll talk about Professor Boonsa. He taught math...or tried to. Boonsa was a VERY animated man of Asian descent. Why do I bring up his race? Because he had a pretty thick accent and, as animated as he was, it was sometimes hard to understand him. The man was practically a Looney Toon. One day he stopped lecturing us so that he could tell us a story about dog-sitting for a friend of his. Apparently this friend had two dogs, a big one and a little one. When Boonsa took these dogs out to walk, the big dog would occasionally pee on the little one. You'd think sharing a story like that in a math class would be odd, but by this point we were used to Boonsa. He then proceeded to draw a picture on the blackboard of the two dogs, so we could better understand what he was describing. Let me reiterate, my math professor took time out of class to draw a picture of a big dog urinating on a little dog. You'd think this kind of activity in a math class would be odd, but by this point we were used to Boonsa. So many of my friends didn't believe the sorts of things Boonsa would do while teaching, so I snuck my camera into class and recorded video of him in action. I wasn't as stealthy as I thought I was though, and Boonsa caught me. Upon seeing me film, he began waving at the camera and putting on a show. I honestly didn't have the heart to tell him that the camera wasn't recording any sound, he seemed really into his one act play.

Moving on to history with Professor G. Now, Professor G wasn't called that because he was cool, or hip, or down with the 411, or whatever slang term is used to represent a relative degree of pop culture acceptance. No, he was called Professor G because his accent was so INSANELY thick that when he announced his name, all we heard was "Professor fwieojGwueri" See the capital "G" in there? Yeah, that's the only sound we could make out for sure. Now, I'm not a big note-taker, never have been, which is something we'll address later, but I HAD to take notes in this class. The fellow sitting next to me and I had a system. Any time one of us heard a word we understood, we'd write it down. The other person would check to make sure they'd heard the word too. Afterwards, we'd try and piece together what it is he was telling us. I've dug through my old notebooks, and I will now share with you my notes from Professor G's first lecture.

Columbus, blue, Nazi, discovered America, green, nuns, Starship Enterprise. He also shouted out "a herd of mamas some of which were horses". Now I realize that he could have meant llamas, or mammals, but he followed this statement up by yelling out "I LOVE MY MAMA". So there goes that line of thinking.

He regularly would spout out odd phrases that I doubt would have made sense even if I could have understood what he'd said before or afterward. Here's a few of my favourites, and remember, I can't give you context for them, because I had none.

"Guinea pigs don't taste bad." "I killed 5 people" "Sea grapes are good" "She wants some bacon" "That's why we buy diet cola". "We need 15,000 slaves" "I'm the lord of Denton" "I'm choosing my words carefully, like your children." "I AM THE KING OF PUERTO RICO!" "I will have no little bastards running around." "Two of my seven kids look like that guy or that woman." "The French were interested in grabbing themselves."

Yes, I was paying large sums of money for this education. Luckily, when so many people in the class failed, the university gave us all C's and told us to keep it to ourselves (which I have just now failed to do). To my knowledge, that was Professor G's only semester teaching.

Now, let's divert from the deranged to the incompetent. Some of you may remember that I majored in film, but you had no way of knowing that I minored in philosophy. I loved taking the classes so much that I made it my minor. But not all of them went well.

One of the classes I was most looking forward to was the ethics class. I pictured rabid debates on morality, ethics, good, evil, and everything in between. It was going to be a utopian learning environment for someone like me, who loves to argue and ask questions. Sadly, none of this was to be. Instead I got some graduate student who'd never taught a class before. She made the decision that in her ethics class, we were going to take extra care to make sure we didn't offend anyone. That meant no discussing controversial topics or any hot button issues.

A class about the philosophy of ethics, wherein we will not offend anyone or raise any controversial issues.

This meant that we could not discuss issues like abortion, gay rights, murder, or anything else that anyone might be offended by. "How do you teach such a class that way?" I hear you ask. A very reasonable question. She did it by bringing everything back to baby eating. See, we agreed as a class that baby eating was wrong, and thus we could use it as an example of ethics. It was the ONLY example we were allowed to use, for a semester. Had I known at the start of the semester how things were going to go, I would have claimed to have been raised as a cannibal, and that I found the idea of her vilifying baby eating offensive, just to watch her head explode when she couldn't teach the class.

The worst part? I had friends taking the same class with other professors, and they LOVED it, they got to ask questions, have heated debates, and get very passionate about the subject matter. I got to write several essays on how it was wrong to eat babies. At the end of the semester, when we got to write our anonymous teacher evaluations, I wrote all of this down, and finished with the phrase "please stop her before she teaches again." Since she told us at the outset that her goal in life was to be a philosophy professor, I know somewhere out there right now a class full of students is stuck writing essays about how it's wrong to eat babies. I just hope one of them has the foresight and guts to defend it.

And one last professor, another philosophy professor. Now, this guy was pretty legendary as a teacher. I ended up having him a couple of times, but the last time was really too much. I can't even remember the topic of the last class, all I remember is that one of the required text books was a sequel to The Brothers Karamazov, written by the professor himself.

For those of you who don't know The Brothers Karamazov, it's a famous piece of Russian literature. This man took a famous piece of literature, written in 1880, and wrote a sequel where the main characters flee from Russia and settle down in Texas to become cowboys. Seriously, it's exactly as if you had a professor who decided to write a sequel to Romeo and Juliet where the main characters come back as zombies in love.

And let's not forget, he made it required reading in his class. The idea of reading assignments in a philosophy class is to foster debate and learning. You can argue what the author meant, and how that meaning applies to different situations. It's a lot different when you're discussing something written by the teacher.

"Well sir, I think it's possible that in Chapter 4, the author is trying to tell us that life is a constant, and that death is merely a transition from one state of perception to another, and not the end of anything really." "No, I wrote that part because I hate my mother. Next."

It takes a lot of the fun out of a philosophy course when there are definitely right and wrong answers to everything. All you really end up learning is the philosophical beliefs of your professor, and his belief that he has writing talent to rival that of Dostoyevsky.

Now, I had probably dozens of different professors in the course of my college career, and I don't want to imply that all of them were horrible at their jobs. Most of them were quite exemplary and affected me just as much as these whack jobs. But let's be honest, reading about some of the criminally insane professors I've encountered is much more entertaining than listening to me talk about how a professor helped me discover the meaning of life.

College Wildlife

Seriously, what is it with college campuses and squirrels? No, this isn't the start of a Jerry Seinfeld routine, I'm serious. It's odd enough walking to class every day and passing by squirrels going about their business. If you're on your way to a morning class, you're probably staring at them jealously, knowing that they can sleep whenever they want. If you're on your way home after a long day of classes, you're probably looking at them hungrily because you haven't had anything to eat since your morning dose of ramen.

But several colleges actually make a big deal out of their squirrels. Mine for example had an albino squirrel that was practically deified. He had a name (which escapes me this many years later), was an unofficial mascot, and had his own preservation society. Why the albino squirrel needed a preservation society, I never quite understood. I actually managed to SEE the albino squirrel a couple of times, which is more than most of the members of the Albino Squirrel Preservation Society had.

Now this in itself isn't so odd I suppose. Students are always doing strange things, it's in their genetic coding. Go to College, be weird. It's an immutable law of nature. The odd part is that when the albino squirrel died (of natural causes we were assured, there was an investigation) my college actually paid to have a new one shipped in.

I am SO glad that part of my college tuition went towards the procurement and transportation of a single albino squirrel in order to maintain the university's UNOFFICIAL mascot. Our official mascot was Scrappy the eagle. EAGLES EAT SQUIRRELS. Oh, and trust me, every student at that university thought they were a goddamned GENIUS by saying that Scrappy probably ate the albino squirrel. I got to hear that stupid joke a good 15 times a day for WEEKS!

But it's not just my school that had squirrel fever. Thirty miles away at my girlfriend's college, trouble was brewing with the squirrel population. See, apparently the psychology department had a fun little activity they performed every semester for incoming freshman. They'd capture a small sample of the squirrel population, shave their tails, and release them back into the wild. Other squirrels that saw their stricken brethren would assume some sort of illness was responsible for the bare tushy, and shun them.

When the squirrel community shuns you, it's not very pleasant. It's a bit like being the one special-needs kid on an elementary school playground. There's taunting (squirrel taunting, if you can imagine such a thing) and the throwing of small rocks.

It was a peculiar thing to witness, but this bizarre

form of animal abuse ended up having a much darker result.

Apparently the squirrels eventually began to catch on that illness was not responsible for this plague upon their society, it was MAN. I swear I'm not making this up, I'll take a lie detector test. The squirrels at this university actually declared war on the student body.

I'd be visiting my girlfriend's campus, and the squirrels would start throwing rocks at you from the trees. You'd be eating lunch in the quad and they actually throw rocks, dirt, or bugs at your food. You'd be walking to class, and they'd run in front of you to try and trip you. These weren't rabid squirrels, they never bit a student, it was strictly guerrilla tactics. The ONLY logical conclusion is that the squirrels had realized that any one of them could be taken away by MAN and turned into a science experiment. They were striking back for the squirrel brothers that had been lost, and to try and prevent generations of future squirrels from suffering the same tragic fate.

It was, quite frankly, damn odd. To my knowledge the squirrels never took a human life, but we may never know for sure. While I rarely wonder what ever happened to that girlfriend, I frequently wonder if the university ever suspended its squirrel abuse, and whether or not the squirrels and faculty met under a flag of truce.

Or maybe the war continues to this day. Just between you and me? I'm totally backing the squirrels.

Of course, squirrels aren't the only form of wildlife to be found on a college campus, there are also hippies!

I wasn't originally going to share this story, it being so odd and pointless. My mind was changed as I came to find out this happens on a lot of colleges, and so maybe this story will resonate with you as well.

When I went to school, there was a girl who was something of a local legend. She was only known as the bare-footed hippie chick. The reasons for this should be fairly self-evident, but just in case, I'll illuminate the situation. She was a female, who dressed like a hippie, and she went around not wearing anything on her feet.

Now, I felt a natural attraction to her, mainly because she was an attractive female and I was a horny teenager, but there was slightly more to it. I've always had a fondness for hippie chicks....I've also had the same fondness for goth chicks, dunno why. I've never dated anyone from either camp, or really befriended them. It just makes me happy to know that they're out there I guess.

I never had the courage to approach her when I saw her walking around campus. After all, she was a living legend, and I was some schmuck flunking history because my professor couldn't speak English. However, during one momentous geology lab, I found myself sitting next to her and I would not let such a rare and beautiful opportunity go by.

I made a point not to learn her name, that would somehow demystify her. It'd be like when you found out what they really put in hot dogs, suddenly they aren't as good. She talked to me for a while about the Frisbee Golf championships that were coming up, and how she kept warm in the winter by not shaving her legs. Finally we talked about her bare-footed ways.

She actually persuaded me to spend the entire next day not wearing shoes. It wasn't hard, she was attractive, I was a boy. So, despite the fact that I'd probably never see her again, I decided to walk a mile in her lack of shoes.

It was...strangely exhilarating. Of course, if you're going to avoid wearing shoes in Texas, best to stick to the grass, asphalt heats up pretty quick. Still, it was a very interesting experience. My feet hurt a little at first, partially because they weren't used to it, and partially (I assume) from a sense of betrayal that I shoved them out into the world without any protection.

I don't know if there's really much more of a point to this, other than to say I think all college students should try it at least once. Break out of your comfort zone for a day and do something weird and silly. It might actually change how you look at the world, even if just for a little bit.

Oh, and I'll pass on a little advice she gave me. Keep a pair of flip-flops in your backpack, in case you need to go into a bathroom. There's being a free-spirited person, and there's being icky.

Funeral For A Friend

This story will probably not be terribly amusing, nor is it likely to be all that entertaining. This story must be told because of the stories that preceded it. Over the course of reading these stories we've bonded, you and I. Although we may never have met, if you're this far along in the book, we're friends. Since we're friends, I think it's important to tell you about a mutual friend of ours.

Daniel, who has featured in many stories, and in many ways was the brother I never had, died in July of 2008, he was 27. His death was sudden and a shock to everyone, although it probably shouldn't have been.

Daniel suffered from diabetes since birth. It was a very severe case, where he had to not only watch his diet, but regularly use medicine to keep his body functioning correctly. It was complications of this diabetes that led to his death, but I'm skipping ahead.

Daniel was my roommate through almost all of college. Even when I briefly moved back in with my parents, I still slept on his couch more often than my own bed. He was always there for me, even when nobody in their sane mind would have been. My battle cry for the longest time was "DANIEL!" to which he would always come running.

Not that I want to paint Daniel as a saintly figure, he wasn't. Some people would frequently accuse him of being a jerk, which he could take a great amount of joy in being. The last several years of his life he was described by some (myself included) as that old man sitting on his porch yelling at kids to stay off his lawn. He hated talking on the phone, was known to yell at people for cooking steak the wrong way, and was a complete and utter slob.

He was also one of the most loyal friends I've ever known.

Daniel was a graduate student in the astronomy department, and he loved teaching. He was a devastatingly bright young man, and that's part of what made his death so baffling.

In the course of my time living with him, I noticed a pattern. About every 18 months or so, he'd get frustrated with his diabetes. He'd seemingly declare that he would no longer be a slave to his disease. He would eat what he wanted, when he wanted, and would take his medicine irregularly. Every time he did this the result was the same, he ended up in the hospital.

There was one week where I didn't hear from him at all. Him disappearing over a weekend wasn't unusual, but when Wednesday came around and he was still gone...that wasn't normal. His phone was turned off, so on a whim I went to the nearby hospital and asked if he was there. I was promptly directed to his room. As soon as I walked in he said "Oh good, I was about to call you, they just discharged me." I began yelling at him. Not only had he done this before, but he didn't even call to tell me where he was. He claimed his cell phone was low on power, and he wanted to save the power for when he was discharged. I yelled at him some more, and he admitted that no, he had failed to think to ask his ROOMMATE to just BRING HIS CHARGER to the hospital.

Daniel was the stupidest smart person I knew. Every time he got out of the hospital, he'd always swear he'd learned his lesson, and then time would prove that he hadn't. Living with Daniel was occasionally frustrating, and when I finally moved out of his place, I needed some space. I barely saw him the next year.

Finally realizing I missed my friend, I called him up to ask him if he wanted to be in another short film of mine (he'd previously starred in several), he was reluctant, but I badgered him into it. He didn't sound well, and he told me he was feeling sick. I told him to take care of himself and got off the phone. He died two days later, and I was the last person to talk to him.

I got a call that night from some friends while I was at work. They hadn't heard from Daniel in a while, and were worried. They had finally convinced the police to break open the door, and he was dead. To this day I still wish more than anything that call was a cruel practical joke.

The biggest problem was that nobody knew where his mother lived. The people who found him gave the wrong last name (she'd been remarried) and wrong city. I knew how to get to her house, but not her number or the actual address. So at 1am I packed my friends up in my vehicle and drove them out to Daniel's mother's house, so we could wake her up and tell her that her son was dead. I hope that this night will always stand out as the worst night of my life, because I doubt I could deal with something much worse.

The only part of this story that remains to be told is the funeral itself. Daniel's mother called me the night before the service to ask me to speak. I had hoped to speak, but finding out the night before? No pressure. Not that I actually bear any kind of grudge, the woman had been through a horrific ordeal, my prep time for a speech was not going to be top of her priority list.

The funeral was PACKED. The entire funeral home was standing room only, from the room itself all the way to the entryway. The physics department of our university rented a bus to ship down students and faculty. People from The Rocky Horror Picture Show arrived in full costume (per Daniel's mother's request). As I said when I started my eulogy, when you pack the funeral home to capacity, you won at life.

I don't care what you think of the afterlife, I really feel like Daniel was with us all that day. First, the funeral director kept calling Daniel by the wrong name. He kept referring to him as David, which was the name of his brother, and also the name of another friend of his who spoke. After getting the name wrong a couple times Leah (who was the leader of Rocky, and basically a Den Mother to us all) stood up and declared "His name is Daniel jackass!" I like to think that Daniel was speaking through her at that moment, except she's always like that.

The funeral director went on to say all sorts of things about Daniel that proved to us they'd never met; we slowly began to get angry. Our anger quickly turned to sadness when they played the bagpipe version of Amazing Grace, and everyone began crying. I was standing in the back with all my friends when a thought shot through me like a bolt of lightning. I said aloud to those around me "You know, if Daniel's watching us right now, he's thinking 'bunch of pussies'". That broke the tension, and a wave of laughter spread through the mosh pit. Daniel's mother turned around to see me in the middle of a giant circle of laughter, and smiled. She absolutely got it.

Now my whole life I've used humour as a defense mechanism against life. Whenever things got too much, I would just start laughing. My philosophy has always been that in moments of extreme stress/sorrow/pain/whatever you really only have two options, laugh or cry. I pick laugh every time, it's not like any of us are getting out of life alive, might as well have a couple chuckles along the way.

This event hit me harder than anything I'd ever encountered. In some ways I doubt I'll ever fully get over it, but I've learned to move on as best I can. When he died there were only two jokes I was capable of making, as distressed as I was. I made them frequently, and to anyone who would listen, and I'll share them with you now in an attempt to bring something a little uplifting to this whole depressing episode.

The first pertains to the fact that he was reluctant to be in another film of mine. My joke was that he really could have just said no, instead of taking the hard way out.

The second joke had to do with the fact that the funeral home was across the parking lot from a hospital. I postulated that it probably saw a lot of business, since the first rule of business is location, location, location.

I realize they weren't funny jokes, but it was the first time in my life I didn't really have anything funny to say.

I suppose if there's going to be any point to this story at all, beyond simply sharing my grief, it's the following. Had I known he was going to die, I never would have spent that year away from him. But that's the point; we never know when something like this could happen. That means it's extremely important to make sure that the people around us know how we really feel about them. You never know when you're going to run out of time, you should tell your friends and family NOW how much you love them.

Go ahead, I'll be here when you get back, I promise.

A Deep Cold Sleep

Ok now, this is one of those things that sounds a lot worse than it actually is. I'm going to tell you about the time I slept with a gay man. I only ask that you hear the whole story before you go leaping to conclusions.

I've played video games most of my life, and while I can't describe myself as a hardcore gamer, I do enjoy occasionally wasting my time in some fictional world or another saving humanity, or fighting some great evil, or just killing zombie Nazis.

When I was in college, the Wii came out. The latest in a long line of Nintendo consoles, and I decided to get one at a midnight launch. I'd never really gotten anything at a midnight launch before, mainly because there was no way I was going to explain to my parents why I HAD to have something the SECOND it was available, rather than sensibly waiting for the prices to come down.

But I was in college now, living on my own, so I could experience such a thing if I wanted to. I invited my

Imaginary Friend Russ to join me, back when he was significantly less imaginary. Russ and I have always bonded over video games; they've constituted 90% of our friendship. In fact we never would have had a friendship at all if we both weren't huge fans of Earthbound.

Russ and I went to our local Target to get us a couple of Wiis at midnight. Even better, the line was being organized by an employee of the store, who knew exactly how many were coming in. You asked him to put your name on the list, and then you waited until midnight, and you were GUARANTEED a Wii. We only had to wait for 3 hours.

Slight hiccup in the plan. We found out that Target isn't open until midnight. If we wanted our Wii, we had to wait in line until 7am. Well, we were already in line, already had our names on the list, what the hell? We figured we might as well have an adventure. True, I needed to be at work at 9am, but so what? I was young, and the only real advantage of youth is that you are invincible. We were also fortuitous in the fact that I had an inflatable mattress in the trunk of my car. We inflated that thing up, crawled into bed, and failed to sleep.

It was particularly cold that evening, and I didn't have near enough blankets, not having planned for something like this. But the oddest part of the entire affair occurred when Russ turned to me and gave me a line to say. I was a little confused, but agreed. He then performed several lines from what seemed to be several different characters, and then pointed at me. I dutifully said my line, still completely unsure what was going on. He then informed me that we had just performed a scene from The Golden Girls.

I am not ashamed to tell you that we spent the next hour acting out scenes from The Golden Girls. Russ would give me the punch line, and then act out the entire scene, and then I would give the punch line. Ok, I'm a little ashamed, but these things happen. Finally we fell asleep for a couple of hours. That is how I spent the night sleeping with a gay man.

I'd also like to add that I hadn't anticipated how cold the inflatable mattress would get sitting upon the cold, cold ground. When we awoke after a few hours of sleep, we were on a giant block of ice. The chill had worked its way into our bones. I've never known such cold in my life.

I also didn't have enough money to afford a game to play on the Wii, not for another week. Luckily it came with a little free game that I didn't have time to play because I had to go to work. My core body temperature was down by 20 degrees, I hadn't had any sleep at all, and I had to go work with a bunch of screaming annoying children. When I came home that night I found that Daniel had spent the entire day playing my Wii. Bastard.

Yeah, I don't wait overnight in lines anymore, I did it once, and that was more than enough for me. Still, if you want to do it, go for it. Just make sure to bone up on your Golden Girls first.

I honestly wish I could claim that was the only time I slept with a gay man, but it wasn't. You may recall from a previous chapter how I was in the Gay and Lesbian club at my college, and again, for the record, I'm still straight.

One of the events that my college did every year was called the Shack-a-thon. All the campus organizations would build little huts out of cardboard, and live in them for two days. You were allowed to rotate out people, but there had to be people at your shack for the full two days. Somehow (and I'm still not sure how), this raised money for homeless people.

I was there to help build it, and agreed to sleep in it both nights, but you had to sleep at least two people there, so it was me and a gay gentleman who spent the night in a cardboard shack. Now, that's fine, it was for charity after all. The real issue came up when during the first night a group of jocks from a frat decided to knock down the "gay shack" with us still in it.

Have you ever woken up to your cardboard house collapsing on top of you? It's a singularly odd sensation.

Determined not to give up (this was for charity…somehow) the next night I brought out the old reliable inflatable mattress, and we slept on that next to the ruined shack.

How many gay guys do you have to sleep with before you're considered gay? I've got to be close to that limit.

How To Score, Badly

I've always had a way with women. I have a strategy you see. First I fall madly in love with a woman. Then I befriend them, to be close to them. Then I spend the rest of the time I know her in the friend zone. It's not a good way, I'll admit, but it appears to be my way.

But that's not what this chapter is about. This chapter is about an anecdote and some free advice, and it's about school.

You've probably noticed by now that I spell some of my words oddly (provided my editor hasn't changed them all as a way to try and make me conform to American standards). Several of my words have an extra 'u' in them. Colour and favourite being the two most frequent examples. I am not spelling these words wrong; I'm merely spelling them the British way.

How this started? I don't even remember. I've always been a bit of an anglophile, and I do think that the 'u' gives the words a bit of extra flavour (that was unintentional, but

I'm keeping it). Perhaps it's my love of British comedies and ordering books from Amazon.co.uk rather than its American counterpart. See, sometimes books come out in England before they come out in America (especially books by British authors), so if you want that book NOW, you're getting it chock full of British spellings. Whatever the source of my rebellious spelling, it's firmly a part of me now. But most of my life I've had teachers, readers, and even my own spell-check against me on this issue. One particularly notable example was in high school.

I was in a gifted and talented English program, because I'm a modest genius. I was lucky enough that all my friends were there. Alice, who I've been friends with since Kindergarten, Steve, who I've been friends with since the 5th grade, and Erin, who I was friends with through all of high school but who immediately refused to ever speak to me again after we graduated. I'd question her reasoning for that if I actually cared. There were a few others, but those were my favourite three in the class.

One day my teacher had finally had enough of me "misspelling" words, and decided to start docking my grade on essays. I would like to point out that she started doing this without warning or asking me to alter my ways at all. I questioned her about it in class, explaining that they weren't misspellings, but alternative spellings. Shockingly my teacher didn't like her authority being questioned (which is something my friends and I were famous for. Steve and I were well known for making math teachers quit in fits of rage for example). She finally said that I needed to just go with the majority on spelling, and since we were in America, the majority was without extra 'u"s.

I then took it upon myself to do a quick survey of my friends, and being my friends they all promptly agreed that they would start spelling their words the same way I did. This put me in with the majority of the people sitting in my group. It's worth noting that Steve did NOT agree to do it, claiming that while he agreed with it in principle, he was far too lazy to start adding extra letters. Still, I felt that since the teacher's argument was that I needed to go with the majority, and the majority of the people sitting near me was firmly on my side, there'd be no more troubles, right?

The teacher did not take kindly to me taking over her class for this, and the next several essays I turned in featured even more points being taken off for my horrible crimes against spelling. But I was young, and stubborn, and refused to change. Eventually she stopped taking points off. I don't think of this as any major victory however, I think she just got tired of caring. Apathy has ever been one of my greatest allies. Other people's apathy combined with my stubborn nature has awarded me more "victories" than I could possibly count. It's not a great way to win, but I'll take what I can get.

And now, for sitting through that drivel, a little free advice. I have found that on rare occasion, when I absolutely do not know the answer on a test, and can't even guess at what it may be, it is always best to simply write "I am a fish". It seems like odd advice, but I have found that 10% of the time, teachers will mark it correct. Now, 10% is pretty lousy odds, but if you're saving it for questions you have a 0% chance of getting right, it's worth a shot right?

The reasons for this are pretty obscure, but I'll

explain. There is a popular British science fiction show called Red Dwarf. One of the famous moments in the show is when a character is so stressed out over taking a test (that he has failed 6 times before) that he has some weird kind of black-out. In this black-out he scribbles the phrase "I am a fish" hundreds of times before passing out completely.

Those 10% of teachers who were kind enough to grant me credit for the phrase were obviously fans, as I was. I know this because they'd often draw smiley faces next to the phrase, or even "I love Red Dwarf". As shocking as this may be, it turns out teachers are people too.

And now, there may even be a small chance that your teacher read this book, and to congratulate you on your fine choice in literature, they may give you points for the phrase. Maybe if we're really lucky, this book will become so amazingly popular that the odds of that phrase working will go up to 11%. That'd be nice, knowing that I've done my part to further education in this country.

It's a last resort weapon, but when you're completely out of options, what the hell?

Failure and Victory

Now, I've alluded before to how I flunked out of college and subsequently returned, but I think it's time for the full story. This one may not be as entertaining as some of the others, but it does have an inspirational feel to it.

I never questioned the idea that I would go to college. I was raised with the belief that college was what you did after high school. It never entered my mind to question that sequence of events. Considering I spent my entire life questioning things, I find that odd. I've decided to attribute that to the fine job my parents did in raising me.

However, I wasn't very good in school. The reasons for this may surprise you. I'm smart. I don't say this to brag, I'm by no means the smartest person I know, nor do I honestly consider myself a genius. Some guys know that they're good looking, others know they're good at sports, I just know I'm a bit bright.

This caused me more problems in school than you'd think. Through all of elementary school, and part of middle school, I knew the answers. I never studied, I never even opened a text book. I somehow inherently knew everything they were trying to teach me. Sure I didn't have history memorized, but I could pick up on it without reading. Same for most other subjects. My life as a child prodigy seemed well on track.

Then suddenly, the level of education they were trying to press upon us passed by my innate level of education. Suddenly I didn't know the answers, and I didn't know how to learn them. I'd never learned how to study, and trust me, it's harder than it sounds.

It took a couple years for me to even catch on that there was an issue. My grades suddenly tanked, and I became a C student (my school district didn't have D's). Now I was drowning, and that's the worst possible time to try to learn how to swim.

I struggled through high school, and in fact, only barely graduated. The morning of graduation, I had to convince my economy teacher that he should bump my grade up a couple points, so he wouldn't have to deal with me for another semester. It was a very near thing.

Now, I had gotten accepted to college, because I do really well on aptitude tests. It comes back to being inherently bright, even if now I was lacking in the book learnin' that is so vital to school.

My final year of high school I befriended the journalism teacher, Mrs. Rose. I joined both yearbook and newspaper that final year, wishing so much that I'd joined them much earlier. There were some days I got permission from all my other teachers to just spend the day in the journalism room. The fact that they were so eager to get rid of me really should have been a sign.

Journalism wasn't really my thing, writing was. I've always loved writing. Instead of studying, or paying attention in school, I was frequently working on my next novel. The only gift I've ever really claimed is an ability to manipulate words. Words are my bitch. The journalism teacher recognized that despite what my grades said, I was a bright kid, who was good with words.

I mention all of this so you understand when it came time to go to college; I picked journalism as my major, because it's what I thought I was supposed to do next. I never really felt any joy in that department though. I don't really like the idea of telling other people's stories near as much as I like making up my own. The next three semesters went by in a blur. Living away from my parents, having a girlfriend who could stay over without any sneaking or hiding, these things were much more fun than a career in journalism that I didn't really care about.

Hell, every semester I had at least one class that I never even showed up to. Sure, I could have just dropped the class, but for some reason I was much happier throwing my money away on classes that I never set foot in. Suffice to say, for the first three semesters of college, I did not pass a single class. The college, used to this sort of stuff I suppose, booted me out. I was informed that I was suspended for one semester, after which I could return if I so desired.

Now, for the first time as an adult, I began to think about my future. I'm not saying you can't have a successful life without college, but I hated the idea of having college be a failure for me, especially when all of my friends were succeeding in it. Some friends even confided in me that they were surprised it took me a whole three semesters to flunk out.

I thought about what I really wanted to do, what would my ideal job be. The answer finally came to me: my ideal job would be that of traveling storyteller. You see, back in ye olden times, there were people who traveled from town to town simply telling stories. They did it with a flair, and gusto, but it's all they did. In exchange for entertaining the townsfolk, they'd be given a couple of meals, a place to sleep, and then they'd move on to the next town. That would be the ideal life for me. Sadly we don't really have that anymore, so I decided to pursue the modern equivalent...film making. Think about it, these people tell a story in celluloid (or digital 3D these days) and ship it out across the country, so all the townsfolk can see it. In exchange for this they get a grossly absurd amount of money. We've come a long way baby.

I went back to speak to my academic advisor, a woman I'd never met before. I told her that not only did I want to come back to school, but I wanted to change my major to film.

After she was done laughing at me, she explained that our film department was very difficult to get into. It had pretty high standards, and a lot of competition. In order to even qualify to try, I'd have to spend the summer retaking four classes I'd failed, and get 3 A's and a B, minimum. She told me that since I'd never gotten an A or a B in my academic life (apparently elementary school doesn't count) I was wasting not only the college's time, but my money as well.

That was enough, seriously. This woman was judging what I was capable of by a sheet of paper in front of her. She'd never talked to me, she'd never spent any time with me at all, but she thought she knew exactly what I was capable of. Her laughter and scorn were exactly the motivating factors I needed. How dare she! I'd show her, and no mistake.

I took those four classes that summer, and I got 3 A's and a B. I even taught myself how to study, and eventually how to take notes. I went back into her office, slapped my grades on her desk and demanded to know what I needed to do next.

That was the last time I ever saw her. After that I never got anything below a B in my classes. Every time I'd start to slack off, I'd just remember her judging my worth based on a stupid sheet of paper and I was renewed.

I can't say this for certain, but it's possible that she's the reason I graduated college. She certainly played a part in the complete reversal of my grades.

So let me say this to all the slackers and underachievers out there. Knock it off. Show people what you're really capable of. The surprise on their faces is well worth the extra effort. Plus, you can make up your own victory dance and do it in front of your doubters. True, it'll make you seem like a jerk, but at least you'll be a jerk who achieved something.

Prove people who think they know you wrong. I've been amazed to find out that whenever I try to push myself to my absolute limit, I don't seem to have one. I doubt I'm the only one.

A Good Word

This is a particularly short story. The only reason I tell it is because it once made a very attractive woman laugh, so it must be good.

I once was in love with a girl. Ok that's not fair, of the thousands of girl's I've secretly been in love with over the years, I'm going to talk about one in particular. There, much more accurate.

This girl had done the same thing as almost every girl I've ever known, she decided we should just be really good friends. I choose to pretend this is because I'm a hell of a good friend, instead of being undesirable as a significant other.

Another factor that's important to know in this story is that I don't lie. I gave it up a long time ago, because I was too good at it. Lying my way through life wasn't challenging or rewarding, and I do love a good challenge. So I took it the other way, and I don't even tell the little white lies we all tell (I sometimes slip, to be completely honest, but I try).

Now this girl, Kim was her name, was looking for a job. She asked me to put in a good word for her at my place of employment. I promised her I would, because I couldn't refuse her. But I'd never worked with her, and I hadn't known her all that long. Also, at almost the exact same time my friend Princess (yes, that's still her name) had asked me to do the same thing. I'd known Princess for a while, and knew her to be highly trustworthy.

Could I really go to my boss with two letters of recommendation, one for a girl I barely knew? No. But I had promised, so I had to come up with something.

I wrote out Princess' letter of recommendation, and at the very bottom, in post script, I added the following.

"Also, a young lady named Kim has asked me to put in a good word for her, and that word is "bubble". I think bubble is a very good word, say it out loud to yourself. See? It's good."

Neither girl was offered a job.

Smooth Talkin' Criminal

As previously mentioned, I have a way with words. In no area of my life is this more prevalent than when I'm talking my way out of whatever bit of trouble I've gotten myself into.

I've talked my way out of more trouble than any decent upstanding person should ever be in. The reason I've had to do this should be fairly clear to you by now. Whilst I endeavour to be a decent person, I've got a mischievous side that is difficult to control.

And when it comes to talking my way out of trouble, my particular favourite has always been speeding tickets. Allow me to share three little stories with you now.

The first was driving back home from seeing a girlfriend in Louisiana. Now, my leaving the state had been riddled with setbacks. First, we realized one of the keys for the hotel was back at her parent's house, so we had to go get that. In the process of doing so, I popped my tire on her curb, and had to get a new one of those. All of these events led to me leaving several HOURS after I'd intended to. To make up for lost time, coupled with the fact that I was in a foul mood (which her parents always managed to inspire), I was going quite fast. Anytime you're in the triple digits, you're going quite fast.

Going over 100 mph, it shouldn't surprise you to get pulled over. How it went down did surprise me though. The second I was pulled over, I reached into my glove box to get my insurance to show to the officer. The officer got out of his car, pulled his gun, and demanded I get out of the car and place my hands on the hood. Of all the times I'd been pulled over, I'd never had this happen. Although to be fair, I'd never sped quite that dramatically in my life.

The cop quickly investigated my vehicle, only to find nothing amiss. He then began questioning me. I was on the verge of tears at this point, this had been a terrible day, and the officer informed me that as fast as I was going, I wasn't looking at a ticket, but jail time. I told him about everything that'd gone wrong, and how I only wanted to go home, which was still more than 5 hours away. He told me that speeding wouldn't get me there any faster.

It took every fiber of my being not to point out that scientifically speaking, it would. An increased speed over a set distance does necessarily provide a shorter amount of time to travel said distance. Nobody will ever truly understand the extent of the personal struggle I had not saying that to the officer.

The officer let me off with a warning. It took a while to figure out the reason behind this odd stop. Finally, with the help of some friends I managed to deduce that since he saw me immediately go for the glove box, he assumed I was carrying a gun. This probably wasn't helped by my

Texas license plate. If you know anything about Texas, it's that we're issued a gun at birth. I'm guessing he was so relieved that I was unarmed, and felt such pity at this 20-year-old kid crying in front of him, he just sent me on my way. All in all, probably my luckiest day ever.

Another time was on my college campus. I had slept in a little late, and had a test I had to take. I leaped out of bed in my pajamas (which I don't normally wear, but it was cold that night) and sped off in my car. Now, before you go getting weird ideas, I wasn't wearing feetie pajamas, just a large t-shirt (for the large man that I am) and some pajama pants. Desperate to get to class on time I turned down a street I don't normally take, and got pulled over. Turns out I was going the wrong way down a one way street. Also, I'd been speeding. Also, I didn't have my driver's license or insurance on me. Also, I wasn't wearing a seatbelt. Also, there was a dead hooker in the trunk. Ok, that last one isn't true, but seriously, would you be surprised at this point?

I explained to the officer that I was in a rush to take a test, didn't realize the street was only one way, and that I really did have a license, I just didn't keep it in my pajama pants. He ultimately ended up letting me off with a warning. I kept that written warning, even hung it on my wall for a while. How often do you get pulled over for that many things, and not even get a slap on the wrist?

And lastly, a time I lied to a cop. I try never to lie, but we are none of us perfect. I was to meet Princess and her boyfriend for a movie in Dallas. That's about a 45 minute drive, and I left my house with exactly that much time. I'd forgotten all the construction going on at the time. You have to understand, I'm never late to anything. I'm always 15 minutes early, at least. The idea of being late was so against my very nature that it made me a little crazy. In between stop and go traffic, and going 90 mph when I could, I began to concoct a story in case I got pulled over. I did, and the story went thusly.

"I know I shouldn't be speeding officer, and I absolutely deserve a ticket. I only ask if you're going to give me one to please be fast, I can't be late."

He then asked me what had me in such a hurry.

"See, I've had a crush on this girl for a long time, and tonight she FINALLY agreed to go out with me. She's giving me just this one chance to prove myself, and I'd forgotten about all the construction work around here. If I'm late for this movie, I'm going to blow the only chance I'm getting with this girl. I know I was doing wrong sir, please just give me the ticket and let me go before I completely screw this up."

Not only did he not give me a ticket, I really think he was about to offer to give me a police escort. As an aside to that story, I got to the theater within seconds of the movie starting, only when we got in the theater it was packed full. The only seats available were on the very front row, so the three of us agreed to catch the next showing an hour later. The exact same result as if I hadn't sped at all.

Maybe that Louisiana cop was right, maybe speeding really doesn't get you there any faster. Science be damned.

The best advice I can give to try and keep yourself out of tickets is pretty simple. Be very respectful, completely own the fact that you were breaking the law, and don't let him think you expect to get away scot free. It may not always work, but the odds are in your favour.

Leg Touching

The following story is actually adapted from an old posting on my livejournal. I barely remember the night in question, but at the time I considered it a grand adventure. I'm as eager as you are to see how good it is. And now, to tell this story, 22 year old me.

It was days like yesterday that made me want to get a livejournal in the first place, to share my day to day adventures, and yesterday ended up being an adventure. Sit back and let me tell you a tale. Key to this story is the knowledge that yesterday involved an absurd amount of rain, for the entire duration of this story, crazy amounts of rain were occurring. Are you ready? Let's start the story after I've been at work for an hour and a half, it's now about 6 in the afternoon, and the sky looks more like midnight, rain is coming down so hard that we can't see our cars in the parking lot and I expect the wind to pick up my little plastic car and hurl it through the parking lot, something my boss said he'd pay good money to see. Are you there, are you set? Then let the story begin.

Work was slow, I'd had maybe three customers the whole time I was there, so I volunteered to go home early, since I can't stand being bored, and my boss was more than happy to save the company paying me the three bucks I probably would have made for staying three more hours. As soon as I get off I call Myrtle, who I was hoping would come to Grapevine today, however with the immense amount of rain, she decided she couldn't do it, apparently her car doesn't function well on the water at all. I decide that since I'm such a gentleman I'll go home, change clothes, and go get her. I spent enough time at her house, it's time she spent more time in Grapevine.

I get home, and am locked out of the house. Nobody is home, and the power went out, which means I couldn't get the garage door open. I can hear the dog trapped inside the house, but I can't get in. I attempt wading through ankle deep sludge in the backyard, since that door is usually open, to find that even that door was locked.

Finally I decided that I didn't need to change clothes just to go and get Myrtle, so I hopped into my car and braved the elements to go and fetch the lovely maiden, and to free her from the tyranny of boredom. The drive was fairly uneventful, but slow. Apparently some lightning knocked out a couple of street lights, bringing traffic to a crawl about ten minutes from Myrtle's house. Her dog was freaked out by the weather, but the true freaking didn't happen until Myrtle was in my car riding to Grapevine. Apparently my wild and crazy driving wasn't enough to inspire confidence. So after we got back to my house and she'd stopped crying, we watched a movie and some Freaks and Geeks.

Then, around 2:15 in the morning, it was time to drive her home. By this time the rain had subsided a little, but the damage had been done. We get to her neighborhood, and the usual path in is completely blocked by water, so we decide to go a little bit further down Northwest Highway and find another way in. While driving down we see the way back to Grapevine on Northwest Highway is flooded, and a cop is preventing any brave but brainless drivers from becoming divers. We finally find a way into her neighborhood, but we come up to another giant puddle. There is a flood gauge, and it's only at setting 1, but it's at the very edge of the puddle, and Myrtle assures me that the road dips down, and it gets deeper.

At this point we decide to wade out and find out just how deep it is. We're both in shorts and sandals, so it's not that bad. We encounter three kids wading from the other direction, two guys and a girl with a cool hat. They had driven through the puddle an hour and a half before, and the water had gotten into their engine, so they were waiting for a wrecker. We chatted for a bit, cracking jokes and figuring out a plan. Myrtle's house is just around the corner, so she could have walked home, but I wasn't sure I could find a way home since the only one I knew was flooded, and I didn't want to leave my car sitting in the middle of the road. At this point one of the kids yelled out "Something just touched my leg!" Of course we all laugh at him for being a complete and total pansy, while we quickly all get out of the water before whatever touched him touched us.

We found another back way to Myrtle's house, the whole time she's practically wetting herself at the thought of going back and getting to know these kids better. So we grab her dog and walk back down there. They were nice, but the girl was going to be in deep trouble when they got home, it was her car, and she wasn't supposed to be out. I decide that it would probably be best to sleep in my car rather than try and drive home. Myrtle decides that the couch may be a better idea, and I'm forced to agree. That night will forever be burned into my memory. (Note from 28-year-old me: No it isn't, I'd completely forgotten this night.)

It's now 5ish, and I'm laying on a couch that smells heavily of cat pee, listening to the LOUD rapping sound of rain hitting the skylight above my head. Sleep doesn't seem likely. From somewhere in the house comes the bizarre sound of some kind of animal being killed, it was loud and terrifying. I wanted to jump up and check to see that it wasn't Myrtle or her dog, then I remember that there were cats, and that might have just been my first time to hear a cat with a hairball. I start to drift off to sleep. Then in the kitchen, I hear a loud crunch and a whirring sound that gets so loud I'm convinced it's going to wake up everyone in the house, and at this point Myrtle is the only one who knows I'm there. It sounded like a blender with a megaphone turned on. The sound eventually died away, and then Myrtle came bouncing out to where I was.

I'm calling it a bounce because I was exhausted, and she was all bubbly and upbeat, she was defiantly freaking bouncing. First she informed me that the odd mechanical sound was some kitchen appliance or another that does that every night. Then she tells me that there is a bedroom right next to hers, with a door, and a bed. So I stumble in there to go to sleep. Myrtle came in two more times over the next ten minutes or so to let me know she couldn't sleep, neither could I, because she kept coming in. Her dog jumped up on the bed with me each time and got comfortable remarkably quickly in the hollow behind my legs, you know, where the knees bend. She was so cozy that I hated to move her, and might not have had Mel not been desperately trying to get her back into her room.

Finally I think Myrtle must have dozed off, it's now around 7 in the morning, and Casey, Myrtle's dog, is wide awake. She starts leaping at the gate separating her from the rest of the house, desperate for Myrtle's dad to let her out. Then she comes into my room, licks my face to wake me up, and then tries to get me to open the gate. I shut the door firmly and went to bed, finally.

I told you it was an adventure, it was a lot of fun, since I'm used to not sleeping well even the bizarre midnight antics of Myrtle's house were enjoyable. Thank you for listening to my story, I'll see you guys around.

Wow, you'd really think an adventure like that would stick in my memory better. It really makes me wonder how many other wonderful events have gone forgotten over the years. Getting old sucks.

Steve the Criminal Genius

My friend Steve is a genius. I know that word doesn't carry around the weight it used to, but I absolutely mean it in the most literal sense. It is highly probable that Steve is the smartest person I've ever met. And my friends in general are no intellectual slouches. Princess is a lawyer who graduated top of her class from law school. Gary is working on his master's in philosophy. Daniel taught physics. Even I'm fairly bright, I mean, I write stories about socks and farts, so I've got to be up there right?

Tragically, Steve is an evil genius. He has a severe penchant for pranks and gags. Of particular note is him changing all the passwords on my computer while I'm asleep, from a secret remote location. Even to this day anytime I have a problem with my computer, I have to stop and wonder if Steve had a hand in it.

He's also quite a persuasive person. To this day I'll never understand how he talked me into spending hundreds of dollars on a present for a girl I didn't really like that much. Or how he convinced me to spend an entire day moving rocks around for his Eagle Scout project, when I wasn't involved in the boy scouts at all. This is a man capable of just about anything.

There is one simple reason that we aren't all currently living in the United States of Steve. Steve is one of the laziest people in the world. There is no doubt in my mind at all that Steve is perfectly capable of building some kind of orbital death ray, and holding the world hostage with it. But that would require him to get off the couch, and there's still stuff on Netflix he hasn't seen. I once asked him to build me a time machine, and he confidently announced that he was all over it. Turns out, his plan for building a time machine was to wait for Future Steve to come back and give him the plans. See? Genius. Lazy.

But this story isn't about any of that, so I'm glad I took the time to tell it all to you. This is the story of Steve, me, and a group of people I don't remember going to a movie. We were going to see V for Vendetta, and we were running late. I still haven't seen the beginning of that movie. On the way Steve realizes that his car needs gas if we have any hope of actually arriving at the theater. So he prepares to do a speed fueling that would leave Nascar technicians weeping in shame.

And in the process managed to pour gas all over himself.

Who said geniuses can't be stupid?

Refusing to be deterred from our course, we hurried onto the movie theater anyway. Although minutes into the ride we realized there was a problem. We were all getting high, and headaches, from the gas fumes pouring off of Steve. I don't know how much he spilled on himself, but it smelled like he bathed in it. We all roll down our windows, and Steve speeds up, hoping that the open road will somehow suck the gas fumes off of him.

We arrived at the theater late, as previously mentioned. There was no chance of any of us sitting together, so we all spread out and found individual seats. The movie was going well, until I noticed a commotion down around where Steve was sitting. Slowly but steadily the people sitting near Steve were walking out of the theater. Had I been more mathematically inclined I'm sure I could have derived great joy from calculating the rate of gas fumes spreading in direct relation to the increasingly large area of empty seats around him. In a surprisingly short period of time, the stench had filled the theater completely. Those that rode in with him were desperately trying not to laugh.

We managed to sit through the whole movie, although at least half of the audience couldn't. When we left the manager was standing outside the theater door. We all figured that the jig was up. Somehow we were young enough to believe that there would be dire consequences for our actions that evening, even though we had in fact done nothing. Instead, the manager was handing everyone who came out free tickets and apologizing for the smell. The reek of gas was so pervasive at that point that he couldn't even recognize that Steve was patient zero for the stench. We all smelled equally of gas by that point.

Steve spent days convinced he was going to get hauled to jail for some reason. And as a gesture of friendship towards him, I have completely changed his name everywhere it appears in this book. You'll never catch him coppers!

Luckily this was before 9/11, because I'm pretty sure what he did would count as terrorist activity. I know I felt terrorized the whole way home, being endless assaulted by the unrelenting smell of gasoline.

Youthful Enthusiasm

I will never, ever, understand how this started, but Kyle and I used to regularly beat the snot out of each other. Maybe it's because he saw Fight Club, maybe we were just stupid. But from time to time, we'd just decide to pummel each other. There was never any rancor involved, nor hurt feelings afterward. We just got a rush out of doing it.

We even had a favourite song. Keep Them Separated by The Offspring. Our fights became almost a choreographed thing. During certain musical passages we would circle each other, and when the beat came back we'd rush forward fists flying. It became a spectator sport for our friends.

Now Kyle was smaller than me, but he also had the speed advantage, so I feel like we were decently balanced. The problem is, that song came on a lot back then. We'd be at the mall, and it'd come on over the loudspeakers, and then suddenly one of us is getting thrown into a clothing rack. It was a perilous time to be around us.

My favourite fight wasn't the one in the parking lot of where we worked. It wasn't the one that wrecked most of an American Eagle Outfitters and left us fleeing from mall security. It wasn't even the one we had outside while my girlfriend was visiting her ailing grandmother. My favourite fight is the one I'm about to tell you about.

It's my school's homecoming dance. Kyle didn't go to my school, but attractive women did, so he was there. We were actually surprised to run into each other, and even more surprised when the DJ started playing OUR song. We looked at each other, dressed up all nice for the evening, surrounded by people, and simultaneously gave each other a look of "what the Hell?"

The fight was on.

Quickly an area clears around us as people watch this large guy and this little guy fighting. Some civic minded members of the football team decided to even the odds and protect Kyle, so they jumped in attacking me. Kyle, true friend that he was, then turned and began attacking them. I've never seen a group of people more surprised. So now the punches are flying, and most people can't figure out who they're supposed to be aiming at. Kyle and I are now fighting back to back against the football team, who honestly didn't know what side they were on anymore.

At this point the Principal had noticed our little scuffle. I'm sure it wasn't because everyone was watching in absolute confusion. He made the unfortunate choice of having the DJ stop the music before breaking up the fight.

Deprived of our fight anthem, Kyle and I came quickly to our senses. The song had stopped midstream, that couldn't bode well for us. In the ensuing confusion I feel like I almost teleported to the other side of the dance hall, where my dear friends Alice and Steve were. They were willing to vouch that I'd been there the whole time. Kyle had a much simpler plan. He simply turned around, found the closest cute girl, and started dancing with her. I believe they went home together later. Kyle always did have a way with the ladies.

This left a very confused group of football players alone to face an angry Principal demanding to know why they were fighting in the middle of homecoming. Looking back, it would have been worth getting in trouble just to hear their explanation. Even if they'd been able to identify us in the crowd, I'm not sure how much good it would have done. Who would believe that two friends like Kyle and myself would get into a fistfight for literally no reason? What could possible cause two people to do that?

No seriously, I'd like to know, it's all a mystery to me these days.

It's been well over ten years since those days, but whenever I hear that song, my blood still pumps harder, and I wish I had a friend nearby to beat up. Still, growing up means not getting into fist fights with your friends for no reason…right?

JEFF HILLARY

You Always Threaten The Ones You Love

I've had a lot of friends in my life, but the title of Best Friend has always meant something to me. It's the one person you count on the most. The one person you know has your back in life. So why is it that two of the three female best friends I've ever had have pulled knives on me?

Alice and I have been friends since Kindergarten, and she was my best friend through most of High School. She was also one scary mamma-jamma. This little 90 pound girl inspired fear in almost everyone who didn't know her, and most of those that did. It had nothing to do with her freaky strength. She played tuba in the marching band, that sort of thing will give you some muscles. It's what caused her to be able to pick me up with no trouble.

But it wasn't the strength, it was her mere aura. There was just something about her that made you believe that not only was she capable of burning down the school after trapping everyone inside, but that she was very close to being able to do it just using her mind.

She was also a very loyal friend. She has long since grown out of being the scary girl who could probably beat you to death with the chain on her anarchy wallet, but the tales of a soccer mom aren't really that interesting.

Now I've changed Alice's name to protect her so I could address the following. Alice had some serious depression issues back then. The only thing more impressive than her collection of lighters (so she could play with fire, obviously) was her collection of knives, some of which she would use to cut herself.

Now this is a serious issue, and I'm not going to make jokes about it. I will just say this much, if this is something you struggle with, you need to be open about it to your friends and/or your family. You need help, it isn't normal, and you deserve better from yourself.

To that end, shortly after she started dating my friend Steve, he took away all her knives. I was also recruited to keep an eye on her, a task I took very seriously. So one day while we were hanging out, it was time to play with fire. Alice had a fun trick where she could use a knife to jiggle some part of a lighter, causing it to shoot out a three foot flame. It was always a crowd-pleaser. But with all her knives confiscated, it was clearly not on the menu for us that night….until she pulled out a knife from a hidden place in her room.

Now I loved Alice, and we were very close friends, but the girl still scared me. I knew how important an issue this was though, so I summoned up all the courage I had and prepared to confront her for the first time in my life.

"Ummm...I think...uhhh..that I'm...uhhh...supposed to...I don't know...ummm...take that from you?"

She glared at me as one would glare at gum on the bottom of their shoe and ordered me to put out my hand. Now I'm no idiot, I knew that nothing good could come of me obeying that command, and I steadfastly refused. She ordered it again, with more force. I still knew that this was the wrong thing to do, and that I could be putting my life in danger. But, while I was thinking about all this, my treacherous hand flew out in response to her command. I still maintain that it did so with no instructions from my brain. And then with one swift motion, Alice sliced her knife across my open palm.

That's when I learned why Steve had let her keep this particular knife. It was too dull to actually cut anything.

I really think there was a better way she could have communicated this fact to me.

Many years later, Daniel and I were living with my friend Jess. Jess is a truly marvelous creature. But again, not someone you want to be on the wrong side of. She's the kind of friend who would not only take a bullet for me, but would then leap at the attacker and beat him to death with his own gun before she decided to start bleeding.

I really should examine why I keep befriending women like this.

Now this story is much shorter. One day I received in the mail all four seasons of Lexx, my favourite TV Show. It's an obscure show that most people haven't heard of, and it actually took me a while to find the fourth season, so I was excited. REALLY excited. So excited in fact that I ran into the kitchen where Jess was, screeched something about Lexx, caught her in a giant bear hug, and spun her around a few times. That's when she reached out and grabbed a carving knife.

Now she didn't come at me with the knife, but she made it absolutely clear that the knife would remain between us for the rest of my giddiness. I knew for a fact that particular knife WAS sharp enough to cut, and so took my exuberance elsewhere.

Jess has since made me two promises, both of which give my life a little extra meaning. First, if my death is caused by another person, it will be avenged. Second, she will not be the person who causes my death. Some of you may be a little worried if a friend of yours promised not to be the one who kills you, but I've decided to take her generous offer at face value. Thank you Jess.

I have been explaining to my current female best friend The Princess that she has a long and proud tradition to hold up, but so far she's been a disappointment. The Princess is not a violent person, nor do I think she will become one. Still, she pulled a spoon on my a couple days ago, so we may be making progress.

The Thanksgiving Massacre in Four Part Harmony

Let's take another trip with 22-year-old me, via the magic of livejournal. This particular adventure occurs over a Thanksgiving weekend.

Ok, I'm going to go over the events of my life starting Wednesday, even though I already kinda covered it, just because it'll flow better that way, I'm going to go fairly fast because I've got work to do, and I'm sick. There are no great stories to tell, just a brief recounting of events. Days will be divided into paragraphs for easy reading.

Wednesday, went to class, a friend in class wanted to know why I wasn't talking to her...like at all. I just couldn't focus on anything other than the fact that Myrtle was coming into town in a matter of hours. I went home to take a nap that was interrupted by a phone call of course. Then I drove from Grapevine to DFW Airport to pick up Myrtle. Pay close attention to where I drove when, I went through two tanks of gas this weekend, it's madness.

Drove from DFW back to Grapevine to...ahem...hang at my house for about 3 hours, then I drove her to Dallas. Visited with her family briefly, and then left fairly early and drove back to Grapevine by myself so she could be reacquainted with her precious doggie. I knew how this weekend was going to turn out, so I got to bed around 11ish, and politely requested she refrain from calling me, which she did, although apparently it was a close call a couple of times.

Woke up about 9:30 Thanksgiving day, did the normal morning routine, shower, internet, that kind of thing, then drove from Grapevine to Dallas to pick up Myrtle for a 1:30 Thanksgiving dinner at my parents. Being the Hillary house there were a few minor disasters, not the least of which being some severe drama in my sister's relationship. So my mom was yelling at Amber a lot, and then the sink backed up. Myrtle and I watched some of Hook on TV, had dinner, and then I drove us both to Dallas to have a 4:30 dinner with her family...and there was a lot of them. Dinner didn't actually start until about 6ish. Several times I was asked by various family members how the two of us met, I let Myrtle take that one, it's her family. Had our second Thanksgiving dinner, and if Myrtle would be so kind to remind her step-mother how much I enjoyed her cooking the next time they speak, I'm going to go and remind my mother how much Myrtle enjoyed hers, because I forgot to. So then I drove us from Dallas to Denton to hang with Daniel and partake of Thanksgiving dinner #3. We hung out in Daniel's apartment by ourselves for a while before and afterwards, we never have enough quality alone time I feel. Then I drove her back to Dallas, and then I drove back to Grapevine. I got to sleep about 1 or 2 in the morning.

Woke up at 5 on Black Friday, and worked...it was horrible, as it always is. For a while I forgot how to breathe, then my knee stopped working, it was just general bad times. Then I got off work, changed clothes and drove out to Dallas to hang with Myrtle for a while. She drove us to Froggies to visit old friends, and got me some glass-bottled Sunkist, which makes me most happy. Myrtle did her fair share of driving my car this weekend when I simply was too tired to drive all the time. I appreciate that greatly. She also offered to pay for my gas once, but was soundly refused. Then we went back to her house and watched The Lost Boys, drove over to visit her friend Remi. Then I drove us back to Grapevine to watch Goodnight Sweetheart, which she tolerated very well I thought. She was uber-sick at this point, but she was still a great sport listening to me whine about Black Friday all day. Finally ended up leaving my house around 1 or 2ish to drive her back to Dallas and then drive straight back to Grapevine. Ended up falling asleep at about 4ish.

Woke up a little before 8 to go back to work. For those of you keeping track, that's four hours of sleep two days in a row. Then I went home almost took a nap, but decided instead to change clothes and immediately drive up to Dallas. I actually kinda fell asleep behind the wheel at one point, it was bad. When I got there I got to rest for about an hour, then we had some errands to run. She drove us to the mall to get her ring finger sized. Ring size is a very important fact for any boyfriend to know, it's right up there with favourite flower. Then she dragged me into some D&D shop to look at clan books for Vampire: Masquerade. I know several of my friends whom that last sentence made very wistful, they wish they had a chick drag them into D&D stores. Then we went into Gamestop where she dragged me out forcibly when it looked like I might buy a game. Then I forced her to take us to a nice steak house where we had dinner. Then we drove back to her house and took a quick nap before she started getting all dressed up for Rocky. Yes I went to Rocky last night, most of it was painful, but there were enjoyable moments certainly. Left the IHOP afterwards at about 3ish, and we fell asleep on her bed at about 4.

We had to wake up at 5:30, only we ended up oversleeping until 7. She took a shower and finished packing while I snuck into her step-sister's room (it was empty because she doesn't live there anymore) and pretended I'd slept there the whole time. Then we hopped in the car and I drove her to DFW so she could catch her flight, emotional goodbye, drove back to Grapevine and slept until 2pm. I need more sleep, but I have two papers I need to write, I just have to force myself to start and they'll be over remarkably quick. Then I'll have dinner and drive up to Denton.

Good lord, I remember having a lot of energy when I was younger, but seriously? Also, somehow I completely left out the Thanksgiving tradition of listening to Alice's Restaurant, where the title for this piece came from.

22-year-old me doesn't really seem to know how to tell as a story as well as I do, but he was tired, so maybe we cut him some slack. Either way, I think we'll leave old livejournal archives alone from now on, and stick to writing new material.

Semi-Lucid Dream Wars

No, that's not the title of the latest sci-fi blockbuster from Hollywood...although maybe it should be.

I've mentioned before how bad I am at sleeping. It's very hard for me to fall asleep under perfection conditions (and perfect conditions are very rare). Once asleep, I tend to wake very easily. In the morning it's very difficult for me to get out of bed. So much so that I long ago had to get in the habit of placing my alarm clock at the opposite side of my room.

The one area I'm halfway decent in is dreams. My goodness, the dreams I've had over the years. All the grand and fantastic adventures that real life has denied me are played out in my dreams. Sometimes my dreams become a mish-mash of pop culture references that is so deep it even takes me a while to unravel. Best of all, sometimes I lucid dream.

Now, for those of you who aren't aware of lucid dreaming, it's a fairly simple concept. It happens when you

KNOW that you're dreaming, and thus are able to change the dream in any way you so desire. Your dream becomes your own personal playground. Talk to long lost friends, fly around for a while, and get the girl of your dreams, all at the same time.

The problem is, my ability to lucid dream has always been pretty random. The worst part is within about five or ten minutes of achieving a lucid dream state, the dream world starts to fall apart and I wake up. When I was in college I decided to experiment some to try and enhance my natural ability to lucid dream. It didn't go well.

I get a very strong feeling that my unconscious mind did NOT want me taking over my own dreams. I had sneaking suspicions before I started experimenting. The fact that my lucid dreams always dissolve so quickly, and the fact that I don't get to have sex dreams. Well, more accurately, I ALWAYS wake up before the sex part of a sex dream. It's really kind of cruel.

But when I started experimenting, trying to gain greater control over my sleeping mind, things went south fast. I'll describe a few of the tactics I used; maybe they'll work better for you than they have for me.

The first key to lucid dreaming is to develop a trigger. Something that will work as a sign to you that you are dreaming. The process of developing a trigger isn't easy, but I had a bit of a head start in that one too. There are two things that are a constant in my dreams. While I may not encounter these facts in every dream I have, they are always true. I can always breathe underwater, and I can never dial a phone.

I don't know why, but any time I push a sequence of numbers in a dream, it never works right. The numbers NEVER come out in the order I want. I thought this would be an ideal trigger. I just had to develop the habit of regularly dialing a phone number and when I got it wrong, I knew it was a dream. My brain had other ideas. I had a lot of dreams where I'd lost or forgotten my phone, which meant I didn't get the opportunity to find out if it was a dream before I woke up. See, the problem with triggers is that they HAVE to happen in order to work. When my brain denied me the chance to dial, I couldn't really go "AH HA! In real life I'd never forget my phone, thus this is a dream." No, the trigger was the act of misdialing, not forgetting my phone. My brain was outsmarting me.

I tried another method. As I went to bed I repeated to myself over and over again in my mind that the very next time I was out of my bed, it was a dream. The next thing I experienced that wasn't in my bed HAD to be a dream.

For the rest of that week I dreamed every night that I was on a magical traveling bed, and I never got out of it.

This was war, and I was on the losing side.

Shortly after that my dreams became very mundane; it was all standard day to day activities. I dreamed about going to school (with all my clothes on), going to work, I even dreamed about trying to go to sleep at the end of a long night. My brain was punishing me for trying to change up the system by taking away the only part of sleeping I enjoyed, my dreams.

So I decided to try and change plans. Rather than

increase the frequency of lucid dreams, I instead tried to increase the duration of them when they happened. I did a lot of researching online. By the way, there are a lot of places offering to teach you how to lucid dream in exchange for large sums of money. Lucid dreaming is nice, but it's not worth actual real life money, trust me.

Apparently, when the dream world starts to dissolve like that, the popular method of keeping the dream going is to start spinning in circles. I know, it sounds really stupid, but a lot of places backed it up. They talked about some scientific mumbo jumbo about balancing your inner ear or something.

All I know is I tried it a couple times, and it didn't do anything. I didn't experiment with it too much though, because I knew somehow it would result with me randomly spinning in circles as I went about my normal life. You can only do that so many times before you start attracting the wrong kind of attention.

Ultimately, I abandoned my experiments. It was quite clear that I was up against a very formidable opponent. What man can fight his unconscious mind when he's asleep? Besides, I still get to have really awesome dreams, and on occasion, I still get to lucid dream for a little bit. Also my brain seems to have extended an olive branch. When I have nightmares, which are exceedingly rare, I always have the ability to just wake up from them whenever I want. That seems like a decent enough compromise.

Also, and this might just be me, but I've discovered that if I watch old episodes of The Twilight Zone before I go to sleep, I get the most incredible dreams.

JEFF HILLARY

My Blood Runs Orange

I admit it, I have an addiction.

No, it's not booze. I don't drink. Mind you, it's not like a moral decision or anything, I just don't like the taste of alcohol. In my entire life, I've been mildly buzzed twice, and I just couldn't drink anymore after that. It doesn't matter if it's beer, wine, or hard liquor. I just don't like the taste. I've had many friends declare that it was their mission in life to find something I like so they can get me drunk. None of them have ever succeeded in this mission. I'm perfectly ok with the sober life though.

No, it's not tobacco. I've had a couple of cigarettes in my life, mostly just to freak people out. I never really felt a need to have my mouth taste like that on a regular basis. I once dated a girl who smoked for a while. She was a hell of a kisser, but it was still sometimes not worth the taste of sticking my tongue in an ash tray. Oh, and there's cancer too.

No, it's not drugs. My reality is altered enough as it is.

There are times I can barely cope with life already, the idea of changing the way my mind functions, even briefly, worries me. I've never been high, nor will I ever be. It's not something I need to do, and at least that way I can go through life without ever worrying about the law, or drug tests. Not that they do a lot of drug testing in the film industry. My addiction is Sunkist orange soda. Oh yes, that sweet, sticky, delightful liquid. When I was in high school, I recognized that I had an addictive personality, and to try and prevent trouble later in life, I chose to focus it on something harmless. In my defense, when you're 15, soda is completely harmless. Who could have imagined I'd reach an age where suddenly I needed to limit how much sugar and caffeine I took in? In retrospect I should have chosen water, but Sunkist was just so yummy.

In college I averaged six cans a day. There was one glorious day that I drank an entire twelve pack. I took a picture, I was proud. The running joke with all my friends was that all of my bodily fluids were orange at this point. All of them! After a while I began to worry that it was contributing to my weight (I'm stocky, but not obese, let's be clear about that). My solution was to quit cold turkey. What happened next nobody will ever believe.

I was thirsty constantly. I was taking in twice as much water as I had Sunkist. After 4 days I got sick, really sick. Sick out of both ends sick. My family took me to the emergency room where I was promptly treated for dehydration. Everyone I know has denied that these two things could be related. "You don't get sick from a lack of Sunkist" they've all told me. I'll admit, they could be right, it could be a coincidence, but at least hear me out. Isn't it possible that after drinking 72 fluid ounces of a substance every day for almost a decade that your body will start to rely on it? And I'm not even claiming that its Sunkist itself my body requires, maybe it's the sugar, or the caffeine (yes, Sunkist has caffeine check the ingredients), hell it could be the yellow 6 dye.

The human body is really an amazing machine that even doctors don't fully understand. I've heard many times of people who become vegetarian or vegan for a while, and then years later they have some meat and it makes them sick. The reason is that their body had adapted to not having meat, and freaked out when it was reintroduced. If that's possible, isn't it remotely possible that our body could become acclimated to a substance, and get sick when it's taken away?

Anyway, after that particular scare, I had to come up with a new system.

I now limit myself to 1-2 Sunkists a day. It was a struggle at first, but now I can't even imagine going through six of them in a single day. If it's a particularly momentous day, I'll have 3, and that seems like a bit much.

My addiction is so much a part of me that all my friends are aware of it. On my birthday and Christmas I frequently receive Sunkist from people, and it's the greatest gift I can think of (as are socks). I mean really, if someone took time out of their day to go and spend money on something they KNOW I will not only use, but enjoy, that's a good gift.

And I'll let you in on a little secret: the best kind of Sunkist is the kind that comes in glass bottles. You may think I'm being silly, but try it, you'll taste the difference. A good chunk of my life has been dedicated to hunting down glass bottles of Sunkist, because as soon as I find a place that sells them, they stop carrying them.

There was a gas station on my way to high school that would sell the glass bottles, and I stopped in EVERY morning to buy two of them. One to drink on the way to school, and another to drink while before my first class started. The owner got to know me pretty quick, and when the gas station was bought out by a new company, I was the first customer to know. He let me know that the new company would NOT be carrying the glass bottles anymore, and for the last two weeks they were available, I was given my daily allotment free of charge. Such a nice guy.

There were two places by my college that used to sell them, neither do anymore. For a while the Wal-Mart near my parent's house sold them, also no longer the case. I'm starting to get a little desperate, truth be told. But that's probably enough about my obsession with glass-bottled Sunkist.

Ok, I've already has two today, but I grabbed this Sunkist out of the fridge to check some facts for this story. It's now sitting on the desk taunting me, all unopened and delicious...

If you'll excuse me, I have an addiction to feed.

Oh The Pain

If there's one thing people know about me, it's that I'm frequently loud and obnoxious. If there are two things people know about me, it's that I'm frequently loud and obnoxious and love Sunkist. This is taking longer for me to get to the point than I'd anticipated. If there are 19 things people know about me, it's a whole bunch of stuff and that I have a bad left knee.

It's a fact that's hard to hide. My knee acts up in cold weather, or when rain is coming, or sometimes just when the wind shifts direction. It prevents me from dancing for very long (a real blow to my lifelong dream of being a professional ballerina). It also makes it so that the only time I'll run is if my life is in danger.

When people learn this about me, one of the first things they ask is how it happened. I usually just fob them off with "a bunch of stuff in high school". But I think it's time to finally let the cat out of the bag.

Our story starts in a land of magic and enchantment,

Oklahoma. We were visiting some friends of the family. Can I just say that there is no reason for Oklahoma? Seriously, it's a whole lot of nothing. It's only purpose in life is to be the source of small towns where celebrities can claim to have been born in, and ran away from as quickly as possible. It primarily exists as something between you and somewhere worth being. I'm just saying.

I was 16, and not yet past the age where a great deal of fun could be had running around like an idiot shooting water guns at another idiot. The ingredients for our mishap are simple, a wet wood deck, a new pair of sneakers, and a moron (i.e. me) trying to run really fast from a standing start. My new sneakers slipped on the wood, and I went crashing knee first into a cement pot.

The cut was deep; I remember actually seeing my knee cap. I was rushed to the emergency room, where six stitches were deftly applied. It was the first, and so far only injury I've ever had that required stitches. The pot did not survive.

Fast forward a month or two. My knee has mostly healed up, and I'm standing in the parking lot of my high school. A girl and I are having a conversation. For the life of me I can't remember what the conversation was about, which I suppose isn't surprising considering what follows. The girl has decided this conversation is over and gets in her car. I disagree, and stand behind her car to block her. Calling my bluff she begins backing up her car. Calling her bluff I stand there until I'm forced to either climb on the back or get out of the way, I climb on the back. Calling my bluff she speeds off into the parking lot, doing what feels like 40 mph, but was probably more realistically half that.

Calling her bluff I fall off the car and skid to a halt on one knee. Ok, so that was less me calling her bluff and more me shifting my hands so the keys I was holding didn't scratch her paint job, but the point remains.

There are three interesting facts about this scenario. First is that the girl never stopped, looked back, or cared in any way that I fell off her car. Second is my ability to fall off a speeding car and not tumble, roll, or hurt any part of myself except the one knee I skidded to a stop on. Seriously, it was like an extreme sport or something. Third was that my dear friend Alice witnessed the entire incident.

As I lay on the ground in pain and bleeding, Alice walks over to me to whisper kind words of comfort. To understand this, you have to understand Alice. She's never sugarcoated anything in her life. She'll never tell you what you want to hear, but often she'll tell you what you need to hear. If she'd said something like "Jeff, are you ok?" I probably would have moaned and cried like a baby for more sympathy. If she'd been sympathetic and supportive I may very well still be laying on the ground in that parking lot today, basking in the glow of someone caring about me. But instead, the words she said to me will ring in my ears for the rest of my life, "that wasn't too smart, was it?"

Indignant and with the kind of swagger only a wounded male ego can provide, I leapt (slowly dragged) myself to my feet (one foot) and boldly proclaimed that "well, at least I can make it to the nurse's office!" I took one step, and Alice caught me before I hit the ground again. I amended my previous statement to include "with your help." The nurse cleaned me up, and I went home…where I oddly don't remember my parents reacting to the news at all. Perhaps I didn't tell them, and they were just used to me limping around.

One thing I never really thought to question until this point was, what was the girl's end game strategy? Was she going to get on the highway with me on the car? Clearly I'd managed to piss her off if she didn't even want to stop and check on me after I fell off. But she couldn't have intended to drive me all the way to her house on the back of her car could she?

Forward a few more weeks, I'm at a football game….in my marching band uniform. I was in the Pit in marching band, meaning my job was to lug around all those giant percussion instruments and play them while OTHER people marched. The instrument in question at this particular game was the chimes. For those uninitiated, think of a large number of long metal tubes suspended on a wooden rack, on wheels. Itty bitty little wheels.

At the end of halftime it was our job to move our equipment off the field as fast as possible. The issue is, this particular stadium had a crack in the concrete lining the field. Itty bitty wheels. I'm pushing the chimes along as quickly as I can when the itty bitty wheels hit the crack. I try as hard as I can to keep the chimes from falling over, but they weigh at least as much as me, and my struggles avail to nothing but to ensure I went down with them. My knee, the very same knee, actually managed to bend one of the metal tubes almost in half.

Ever the professional, I hurriedly righted the chimes and got them off the field. That accomplished, I collapsed. The drum line instructor, sensitive caring soul that he was, put the chimes up on display in the band hall. He attached a note to ensure that everyone who saw it knew exactly who had damaged this precious musical instrument. A few weeks later the chimes were given a new frame, and some enormous ATV type wheels. I was not allowed to move them anymore though.

At this point the damage was done, and my knee would never recover from so much trauma in such a small space of time. I spent the next couple years limping most of the time. A couple of runs through physical therapy failed to achieve any measure of healing. Finally I was taken in for knee surgery, which helped a lot, but not completely. On a good day you'd never know there was something wrong with my knee, but if you hang around me for more than a week, it'll come up.

One last knee tale, from years later. I'm working at an office supply store, and I'm moving a LARGE amount of paper. Those of you who've never worked with bulk paper before have absolutely no idea how heavy large amounts of paper can be. I'm moving this large amount of paper on pallet jack (picture a fork lift operated only by hand). While loading these giant boxes of paper onto the shelf (and looking like a 90 year old man doing so) a couple of the boxes fall off the jack. I watch in slow motion as the boxes fall against the handle, causing it to swing low, and at the speed of light, into my left knee. People who witnessed the event claim that the speed that I went from vertical to horizontal defied human imagination.

Do you think it's possible that different parts of use are reincarnated from different people? If so, I think I have Hitler's left knee, and karma's a bitch.

The Ballad of Sue

I'd previously mentioned that I had a way with women, and then promptly explained how it is a bad way. This is never truer than when I talk about Sue.

Guys, do you remember when you were a little kid, and you got a crush on a girl for the first time? I'm not talking about when you were a teenager; I'm talking about on the grade school playground, back before you would consider those feelings a crush. You knew it was wrong, because girls were icky, and had cooties and other such things. Obviously the girl was at fault for making you like her, despite it being wrong, so you threw rocks at her. She had it coming for filling you full of those weird and unfamiliar feelings. With that in mind, let me tell you about Sue.

I liked Sue from the second I first saw her. I actually really wish I could share her last name with you too; her full name is so spectacular that I've been told her husband actually took her last name to keep it intact. Sue was beautiful, funny, quirky, and delightful. It was pretty much love at first sight for me. There was only one problem, I was in a serious relationship, and had been for over a year.

I've always been a remarkably faithful person. I don't even flirt with random people when I'm in a relationship, because I feel it's a betrayal of trust. The idea of having a crush on a girl when I'm in a relationship with another panicked me. I knew it was wrong, and so it must be Sue's fault. So I threw rocks at her.

Not literally, obviously, but I was quite mean to Sue. And because I liked her, I made sure I was around her a lot TO be mean to her. She was hard pressed to escape me, because we were both on the cast of Rocky together, and so was my girlfriend. I never told anyone about my feelings for Sue, in fact this chapter will probably be a shock to most people. But despite me never telling her, I think my girlfriend had an inkling, because she was always badmouthing Sue to me. I can only imagine the sorts of things she probably told Sue when I wasn't around.

It was remarkably unfair to Sue, and she came away from it with the impression that I was an absolute and unmitigated jerk, which I completely deserved. After a while Sue and I didn't see each other anymore, for which I'm sure she was very glad. I was a little sad, especially since my relationship ended not terribly long after that, but I got over it in quick order. I'd almost forgotten all about her, after all, there were so many other girls I had to get rejected by.

A couple years later I see her on my college campus. I'm single now, and one look at her and I'm in love all over again. But now I've got all this damage to undo, and there's an additional problem. I'm not sure if the new problem was completely related to how I treated her in the past, but I had now had the magical ability to piss her off with every word that came out of my mouth.

We tried to be friends, we really did. I tried as hard as I could. We'd hang out for a little bit, then I'd say something wrong and she wouldn't talk to me for a couple weeks. Then we'd hang out again, and I'd say something wrong again. To my mind, the final nail in the coffin came when I went to go see her in an independent film. See, Sue wanted to be an actress, and I wanted her to be in a film of mine, so she invited me to this screening to see her work. The film was called E. She was incredible, the film was incredibly not. My friends that I had dragged along with me all agreed. When later she asked me for my opinion, that's what I should have said. However, I've always believed my foot belongs firmly in my mouth, and when asked I told her that it should have been called E for Effort.

Yeah, it's a cute line, but I think it's the last conversation we ever had. I saw her years later. I was at a movie theater by myself (sometimes I watch 2 or 3 movies in a row, most people can't do that, so I see a lot of movies alone) when she and a boyfriend walked in. The three of us were the only people in the theater. She saw me, said hi, and then they left the theater. They did not return.

This is all a little awkward because over the years she actually developed friendships with two other friends of mine. And as much as I'd love to put our past behind us, she still isn't willing to accept my friend request on

Facebook. You know things are bad when someone isn't willing to be your friend on Facebook. Usually the only requirement is…..that the person request friendship.

How much of this was my fault for my completely immature reaction to my feelings for her? How much of it was just my innate nature innately pissing her off? We'll probably never know. She's not the only girl I've managed to have such a long lasting effect on, but she's the one I regret the most. I hold no delusions or dreams about winning her over; she's married, and from all accounts quite happy. The fact that she lives on the opposite side of the country from me probably helps too.

But while we're on the topic, I'd at least like to take this opportunity to say I'm sorry Sue, you're a swell gal, and I apologize for every verbal rock I threw your way.

Plan B

So I made my first feature film last year. It wasn't my first one to work on, but it was the first one that was all mine. It's a big accomplishment, and it taught me a lot. I could write an entire book on the experience (and I just might, don't test me) but the most obvious lesson is the one I'd like to share with you now.

Always have a backup plan. If possible, have a backup plan for your backup plan. Your primary plan will NEVER work. I have joked many times that I should have called my movie Plan B, because it's the only plan that worked.

Actors' schedules, props, location permission, and everything else you could possibly imagine fell apart the second I arranged it. To my credit, the film got done, because I was always able to come up with a Plan B, usually at the last second. One experience was almost the end though.

Part of the movie was planned to be shot on a college campus. I figured the easiest to get access to would probably be my old college, since they gave me a degree in film, and I'd shot a lot of short films there. The process of getting their permission turned out to be a much more Sisyphean task then I could have imagined. What I'm about to describe took MONTHS of emailing back and forth, and while I began the process in pre-production, the deal was concluded almost too late to actually film.

I told them I wanted to film, they said it would interfere with students and classes. I offered to shoot during the summer break, and on weekends. They then had me make revisions to the script. There's a scene in which a girl flashes, they weren't ok with that. There's a scene with a boom box, they weren't ok with that either, and there's a scene where the characters make a brief reference to Chilton Hall, they weren't ok with that either. There was more, but let's stick with those three shall we? I wrote back explaining that while the script says "she flashes" there is NO nudity, it only looks like she flashes. I also explained that the boom box wouldn't play any actual music, so it couldn't disturb the students THAT WEREN'T GOING TO BE THERE ANYWAY! And lastly, I chose Chilton Hall because after doing research I discovered that the majority of college campuses have a Chilton Hall, and it would add a sense of immediacy to the audience.

The school had me include in the script that the flashing wasn't real, and that the boom box didn't actually play, along with several other notes that are extremely unprofessional in a script. They also insisted again that I remove the Chilton Hall reference, because despite my claims of research, and the list of colleges I gave to back it up, they felt it identified the university too specifically.

They were ok with the fact that we referenced a street that ran alongside the university by name though.

Finally, after all of that, it still came down to getting permission for which days to shoot. I told them I needed 5 days, but that they could pick the days and I'd work with those. They insisted that I pick the days. This felt like a trap, I'd name five days, and they'd say they wouldn't work, but no matter how hard I tried, they wouldn't pick the days for me. Finally I sent them a list of ten days I'd be willing to shoot, and told them I only needed five of those ten. They sent back three days that were acceptable. Luckily, after all this fighting I'd done with them, I had a good idea of what they were about and in truth I only needed three days. All I had to do now was pay the $1000 for insurance to allow me to shot, which is a lot of money to someone without a job.

Now, we're on a very tight schedule, because after these three days we can't return to the campus, so everything needed to go like clockwork, which is really begging for disaster. We were also shooting one of our biggest scenes, with 15-30 extras. Oh man, was I asking for grief.

Let me lay out the scene for you. While walking along the campus our little band of heroes stumble upon a man preaching to a large crowd of students. They have some dialogue, eventually chase off the crowd, and the preacher goes on his way. I had spent a month previously arranging for extras, I had 15 of them confirmed, with more possible.

The day we're shooting this scene, four extras show up. Now explain to me how I'm supposed to make four people look like a multitude listening, enraptured, to a preacher? I am not ILM (Industrial Light and Magic, they make Star Wars look Star-Warsy) and no special effects I can muster will make four look like fifteen. PLAN B! I had my Assistant Director take my scantily clad actress to the frat houses to start recruiting students....there were none. We had gotten permission to film this weekend because there would be no students around.

This was it, $2000, over a month of work, so many favours called in, and my movie was never going to get made. I was done. Then, a tour group walked by. It couldn't have been any more ridiculous if the clouds had parted and a shaft of sunlight lit upon them while a chorus of angels began singing. A tour group filled with people is walking RIGHT BY my set!

If there's one thing I'm good at, it's talking. I think I could sell ice boxes to Eskimos if I needed to. It's not a talent I like to overuse because forcing people into things they may not want to do makes me feel dirty, but just this once, I was going to use this talent for all it was worth. I approached the tour group and asked them if they wanted to be in a movie. I incorporated the fact that I graduated with a degree in film from the very university that they were touring. Somehow I made the logical connection that being in my film would be a natural part of the college experience. After a quick sales pitch most of them agreed. We created an assembly line of getting them to sign waivers and stand in position.

Now, shooting the scene was going to take at least an hour, but I couldn't have made them stand there that long, so it was time to be a filmmaking genius. I stood my four extras at one corner of the crowd, and proceeded to shoot all of the crowd's reactions in a matter of minutes. Then I sent away the tour group. I kept my four to use in the corner of the shot when the heroes appear. This way you can see that the heroes are CLEARLY standing next to the crowd that isn't actually there anymore.

Through the magic of editing, it looks like all those extras stayed for the entire shoot. I suppose the lesson of the story should be "stumble around and then figure out something at the last second to save the day", but I'm going to pretend the lesson is "always be prepared, and always have a backup plan."

Look at that, a little filmmaking knowledge, and I'm not even gonna charge you extra for it.

JEFF HILLARY

The Great Grandma Caper

My grandmother was a great woman. She was the peacekeeper in a large family prone to loud arguments. She's also one of the very few people I've ever heard say the phrase "I don't agree with you, but I respect your right to have a different opinion than me," and actually mean it. She was a matriarch unlike anything you'll find today. I could probably spend several pages extolling the saintly qualities of my grandmother, but I'm not going to. To borrow from a writer so much greater than myself, my grandmother was dead: to begin with. There is no doubt whatever about that.

She lived in Colorado, which has some truly beautiful scenery. Why do I bring this up? Because she wanted her ashes spread amongst that scenery. More specifically, she wanted her ashes spread in a lake that she and her youngest son once went fishing in. High up a mountain, away from almost all signs of civilization. I won't mention the name of the lake, or the names of all the various relatives involved. Nor will I tell you the size of our group, except that it was quite large. I'm withholding all this information for a very important reason: I don't think I'd last long in jail.

When we arrived at the lake, we found out that it was a protected lake. It's protected by some state government organization, none of us were even allowed near the lake without a special permit, which only one of my uncles had. This particular uncle is the only member of the family that stayed in Colorado after graduating high school, and had always been something of a mountain man. Sadly it turns out that his permit was only good for one person. It did not cover a large group of people and a sack of ashes, we checked the fine print. Not that any of this should have mattered, I mean, we weren't going to be there long enough for anyone to call the fuzz. We would walk along the lake, have a dignified little ceremony, dump the ashes, and be home in time for Matlock, or whatever it is old people watch these days.

Except the fuzz were already there when we arrived. This is where our story veers off the path of law-abiding righteousness. I refuse to apologize for this fact though, we were on a sacred mission and one every bit as important and righteous as the one undertaken by a Mr. Jake and Elwood Blues.

The Official Colorado Lake Enforcement People Type Things (Or OCLEPTT as they preferred to be called) where at the lake for some reason I doubt we'll ever know. Knowing that what we were about to do was of...questionable legality...we hid my grandmother's ashes from the OCLEPTT, in a nice jewelry bag if memory serves. Upon seeing our large group, the OCLEPTT approached us to see our permits, which we didn't have. We were instructed to leave the lake immediately, but my uncle asked if we could be permitted to stretch our legs, because it had been a long drive. The OCLEPTT agreed, and we casually stretched our legs until they left, trusting us to be honourable people of our word, and expecting us to depart shortly thereafter. Suckers.

There is no honour when it comes to loyalty to one's deceased grandmother. As soon as they were gone, the plan was back on. There were a few people around the lake, but it was a large lake in a mountainous region. We quickly began walking the perimeter trying to find a spot in the lake where nobody could see us. We knew we had to hurry before the OCLEPTT (or spoil sports, as they prefer to be called) returned.

At last we had found an ideal location (ideal in this case meaning hidden) so we quickly, but as respectfully as possible, poured my grandmother's ashes into the lake. Oh man, was that bad. A little heads up for those of you who don't know: cremated human remains are white. Very, very white. When you pour a large amount of white ash into a lake, it forms a giant spreading cloud of white. Now, in the lakes you guys are probably used to, this wouldn't be an issue. But this is an OCLEPTT protected Colorado nature lake. The water is pristine and clear. Not an ideal situation for HIDING ashes. As my grandmother's ash cloud quickly grew, we became increasingly concerned. There was talk of satellite images and us being arrested as terrorists. There aren't words adequate to explain the sense of dread that blossomed and grew within all of us as we watched my grandmother's mortal remains begin inexorably spreading across the lake. Needless to say we booked it out of there quick.

It was a very nervous drive back down the mountain. For a Texan, driving down a mountain can be nervous enough, but for all we knew, we were on the lam. The tension only alleviated by the fact that all of us knew it'd be a story we could look back and laugh about, provided we weren't arrested by Homeland Security and sentenced to Gitmo. Well I'm here to tell you that our little act of familial terrorism was never followed up on, and all of the parties involved got away with it scotch-free (as my sister likes to say.)

This was about the same time my friend Daniel passed on, so I wasn't in my typical merry mood. Even so, it is impossible not to realize the inherent comedy in the situation. I've said it before, and I'll continue saying it until I die; often in life you're forced to choose between laughter and tears. I always pick laughter. It was truly the Keystone Cops of funeral services. I only hope the disposal of my earthly remains can cause such comedy. I know if my grandmother was watching, she was laughing her ass off.

What Not To Say

There are few friendships I've ever had as deep and meaningful as I have with my friend Jess. In fact, it's difficult to describe my relationship with Jess without it sounding romantic, or as if it should be romantic. Jess and I have never been romantic, nor shall we be (her fiancée would kill me). The short version is, once Jess and I met, we knew we'd found our platonic soul-friend-non-sexual-mate. If ever I was in some kind of street brawl, fighting for my life, I wouldn't be surprised if Jess magically manifested to help me even the odds. I like to think our friendship defies the laws of physics. In the most emotionally tumultuous parts of my life, Jess has always been a little rock that I could secure myself to.

Of course, having a deep friendship like this with a member of the opposite sex wasn't without its teething problems. I was pretty used to the idea of having friends of the opposite sex. In fact, at the moment I only really have about 3.5 close male friends (sorry Imaginary Friend Russ, you're the .5). But at the point this story happens, the idea of understanding and vocalizing platonic love was still a new thing. Hell, the idea of telling people you aren't related to, and that you aren't trying to have sex with (there's an Arkansas joke in there somewhere) that you love them is pretty foreign to a lot of guys.

Let me paint you a terrifying picture. I'm at Jess' parent's house. She and I are watching T.V. She's laying on the couch, I'm sitting normally. She's leaning into my side, and I have an arm around her waist. Once again, no romantic tension, just two friends hanging out. We talk for a little bit, and then tell each other that we love each other. We say this sort of thing a lot these days, back then it was still a new occurrence.

It was right after this that I noticed her father had walked into the room. He'd seen the entire exchange.

My thought process went something like this..."Oh crap, I've never even met her dad before. He knows nothing about me. He just caught us cuddling and talking about how we love each other. He's going to get the wrong idea. He's going to think we're dating. We're totally not dating. Right now he's thinking about how I'm probably having sex with his little girl. He's thinking that I've stuck my disgusting man parts into his pristine little angel. Oh man, just say something! Why did we have to be sitting like this? Talk to the man! EXPLAIN TO HIM THAT YOU AREN'T HAVING SEX WITH HIS BABY GIRL! SAY SOMETHING!" It was one of the only times in my life that words utterly failed to come out of my mouth. After a massive personal struggle, which I'm surprised didn't result in some kind of aneurism, I managed to shout the following in a squeaking barely pubescent kind of voice.

"I'm not having sex with your daughter!"

Now, meeting the parents of someone you're having sex with is a little awkward by its very nature. But greeting a father for the first time by explaining that you aren't boning his daughter is somehow much, much worse. My relationship with her parents has never been good since then. Hard to imagine, I know.

In my defense though, as much as I can defend such an egregious case of foot-in-mouth, I still stand by what I said as a basically positive thing. First of all, it was the truth, I was not having sex with his daughter. Honesty is always a valued commodity right? Secondly, it should have put his mind at ease. If I have a daughter, the more people I know aren't having sex with her, the happier a father I'll be. Seriously. In fact, I'm considering forcing every guy she ever meets to take a polygraph about whether or not he's having sex with my daughter (yeah, being my daughter's going to be a blast.) Third, the only reason for him to really be upset is if he thought I was lying. Does he think so little of his daughter that he believes she would hang out with liars?

If only he'd been an ultra cool laid back sort of dad. He could have looked at me and just said "Neither am I" and we all could have laughed until most of the awkward tension in the air was gone. To the best of my addled recollection, I don't remember him saying anything at all. He simply left the room. A couple years later Jess moved in with Daniel and me for a while. What her father must have thought then.

And by the way, how incredibly rude of this man to assume I'm a liar. He's never met me before, and he's going to assume that the first sentence out of my mouth is a falsehood? I'm offended. His response shouldn't have been a lifetime of dislike, it should have been "Why thank you son for not having sex with my daughter, and being so honest about it. You've set my mind at ease, and I wish the two of you a long and healthy friendship. Consider yourself part of the family."

Jess, tell your father I demand an apology!

On the upside, relations with the parents of girls can only get better from there. Although with Jess' wedding coming up, I'm confronted with the real and growing fear of having to face her parents once again.

Would it be inappropriate, do you think, to reiterate to her father that I'm still not having sex with her? Maybe what he's needed for all these years is reassurance that I meant what I said.

Mathematically Illiterate

I, like many people who can't do math well, play the lottery. In my defense, I have no expectation of winning. I play the lottery (and by "play" I mean give away about $10 a week to the local gas station) for one very simple reason. In the couple of days between purchase and drawing, I get to have some lovely daydreams.

It astounded me to learn that a large number of lotto winners end up with their lives in utter shambles about a year after winning the lottery. How could millions of dollars ruin your life? Easy, they didn't have a plan. In order for that much money to actually change your life, you need a plan.

I'm going to share mine with you now, aren't you so lucky? Make sure to take notes, there might be a quiz on this later. And I won't accept "I am a fish" as an answer...probably.

I'm going to assume we're talking about around $10 million after taxes, because it's a nice number.

The first thing I'm going to do is pay off my student loans. That's pretty much the only outstanding debt I've got, which puts me in the land of having NO BILLS (thanks for the free room and board Mom & Dad!). I would then purchase a new car. That wouldn't go how you think though, I wouldn't go out and buy a Ferrari, or a Lambo, no, something comparable to what I'm already driving. My current car is a Saturn Ion with over 100,000 miles on it. My new car would be similar: something reliable, but far from fancy.

Then begins my "Charity to Others" phase. Because if you're lucky enough to win the lottery, you need to spread some of it around, otherwise karma's going to drop an airplane on your house. I'd pay off my parents' mortgage, toss my sister enough money to set her up in an apartment of her own for a while, and then address my friends. I love my family, deeply and truly, but they have to put up with me. My friends are the people who, for whatever reason, have CHOSEN to associate with me, often of their own free will. This demands reward.

Each of my relatively close friends would get between $5 and $10 thousand, depending on how much I like them, and how much money I actually win. On top of that I would give my old car to my friend Gary, so he and his wife can finally be a two car family. There's actually quite a few other things I'd do to help out some particular friends, but the thought occurs that they may not want their private business aired in this manner, so…moving on.

The next major plan is to sit down with a financial advisor. I'll use the same one my parents used when we had some relatives with cash kick the bucket. That guy didn't run off with their money, and that's something I always look for in a financial advisor. I'd use him to invest the majority of my money. I'd be looking for an investment that paid out dividends around five to ten thousand dollars a month for the rest of my life. This ensures that no matter what I screw up, I've got a nice safety net waiting for me of $60,000 to $120,000 a year. That's a nice safety net.

Now we'll assume I've got a million or two left. First we set aside about half a million. We'll come back to that later. Now it's time to travel. I'd have to apply for my passport of course, but while I was waiting for that, I could travel the USA. Visit Steve in Seattle, Alice in Colorado, Jessica in Indiana, Cody in New York, and spend some time relaxing on a beach in Hawaii. Once the passport arrives, it's a couple weeks in England, a month or two traveling across Europe, a week or two in Japan, another couple weeks in Australia. The trick at this point is going to be staying in ordinary hotels, not 5-star establishments. You'll find me in whatever the European equivalent of Best Western is. By this point I'll be home-sick, and it'll be time to come back and use that half a million to purchase a house in Austin.

I've always loved Austin, so where better to set down some roots? Half a million dollars will buy you a pretty nice house, especially for a single guy. I'd have enough bedrooms for friends to come stay for weeks at a time if they wanted (a lot of my friends love Austin). Hell, I've got a feeling at least one of the bedrooms is always going to be taken up by some free-loading friend or another. Welcome to the Hotel Jeff, you can check out anytime you like, but I bet they never leave.

Then, I'd use whatever money I had left over to start making movies again. Oh, I'm not just going to sit here and enjoy my safety net, I'm going to use it to finance feature films. I could only sit on my butt being unproductive for so long before I went crazy (28 years seems to be about my limit). I made my first feature length film on $2000; I can't imagine what I would be capable of with an actual budget behind me.

I think the problem people have with inheriting insane amounts of cash unexpectedly is that they want to spend is in a grossly lavish fashion. They try to make up for everything they ever lacked in life. This is a very quick way to ensure the implosion of your life. In this, as in most things, moderation is key and planning is essential.

So now all of you have a homework assignment, figure out your plan for how to deal with winning the lottery. And when you reach your "Charity for Others" phase, remember, I could always use money to make another film. I'd give you producer credit…please?

Me and Julia

I like Julia Stiles. I think she's a very attractive woman, and a very talented actress. That said, bitch owes me some ice cream.

Perhaps I should explain a little.

This story involves Kyle, from the Great Platypus Caper and the Long Imagination of the Law. It also involves the Grapevine Mills mall, known to the hip locals simply as the Mills. Now the Mills is no different from any mall you've ever been in, except for the fact that it is laid out as a giant donut. Walking the mall is remarkably simple: you pick a direction, walk for about a mile, and end up where you started.

This is exactly what Kyle and I were doing one day, walking the mall. Now, if you were to ask the proprietors of the sports store, they might tell you that we were in there. They'd probably claim we were attempting to invent new sports by hitting dodge balls with golf clubs, or basketballs with baseball bats. But really, why would a couple of teenagers do such a thing? That's just silly.

The owners of the candy store may also claim to have been visited by us. They'd probably say that we attempted to purchase multiple jelly beans, one at a time. If this were true, it'd be because a single jellybean doesn't weigh enough for them to charge you, thus buying them one at a time tends to get you free jellybeans, until they get sick of you, if this were true. But again, why would anyone spend their time in such an unproductive manner?

The owners of an upscale clothing store might even claim that we were seen fighting in their store. They might claim that our brawl took out an entire sunglass display. But how absurd is that? Kyle and I were known to randomly start beating the daylights out of each other for fun (what teenager didn't see Fight Club?), but doing so inside a clothing establishment? That would be needlessly destructive, and teenagers are well known for their quiet respect of hard-working folk.

Now, the story about me hitting on the Goth chick working the register at Hot Topic? That one was true. But come on, she was hot!

But these spurious stories are not the focus of this chapter. The focus is this, while Kyle and I were walking around the mall (minding our own business and not being a menace to any employees anywhere) we were approached by a woman. She asked if we wanted free ice cream, and of course we did. With that she invited us into the middle of the Mills doughnut.

I can't speak for Kyle, but I didn't know there was a middle to this doughnut. I guess I thought it was some kind of private garden, or top secret government facility. All I knew was that she took us through some doors that said "Authorized Personnel Only" that Kyle and I had never seen (or knowing us, we would have immediately authorized each other and went exploring). Whatever I thought might be in the middle of the mall, I didn't expect it to look like creepy office basement. Low ceiling, exposed pipes and wiring. There were lots of small hallways and doors, including one I'm convinced led directly into John Malkovich's brain.

At this point Kyle and I had a hurried whispered conversation, wherein we admitted to each other that we were being brought back here to be murdered and raped (although possibly not in that order). We weighed this against the possibility of free ice cream, and judged it well worth the risk. Life is cheap, and ice cream is delicious.

Then we were separated and each taken to separate tiny separate rooms. I may be emphasizing the separate part a bit hard, but all of a sudden my bravery about potential murder and rape was halved.

Then a man came in and asked me to watch a trailer for the latest Julia Stiles film. It was some movie about her being taught how to dance by an urban gentleman. They probably fall in love at the end. I'm sure if I spent five seconds on IMDB (a fine website that I wholly endorse, and not just because I'm on it, although mostly because I'm on it.) but I don't really care much for dancing movies. This could be because my knee prevents me from doing a lot of dancing and having other people dancing shoved in my face is a painful reminder of how I'll never be whole. Or it could be because I'm a guy, and guys generally don't like dancing movies. If I had to bet money, I'd place it on the latter rather than the former.

The man asked my opinion about the trailer and my impressions of the film in general, and then released me.

Reunited with Kyle we approached the lady again. Our ordeal was over, and it was about to be rewarded with frosty delicious treats. That's when she told us that they were out of free ice cream vouchers, and instead gave us coupons for free waffle fries from Chik-fil-a.

Let me assure you, waffle fries are NOT a good substitute for ice cream, no matter what the liberal media would like you to believe. It was doubly worthless for us anyway, we were banned from the Chik-fil-a in the mall. For those that don't know, Chik-fil-a ONLY sells chicken related products. The fact that Kyle and I would stop by there every time we were at the mall and DEMAND they fix us a cheeseburger never went over well. Also, Chik-fil-a apparently has a three strikes policy about this kind of behaviour.

So listen Julia Stiles, wherever you are. You owe me ice cream; I was promised it in return for reviewing a trailer for you film. I held up my end of the deal, now it's your turn. You can probably track me down through the publisher of this book. I'll be waiting.

Don't worry about Kyle though, he secretly told me he hates you, and I stopped being friends with him over it. I got your back Julia, and that kind of loyalty deserves to be rewarded with sweet delicious frozen goodness.

Naked and Not Alone

One of the easiest to get, and least glamorous, jobs in the entertainment industry is that of an extra. Anytime you watch a movie or a T.V. show, and you see those people milling about in the background, the ones who never have any lines, those are your extras. Almost every actor out there has done some extra work in their time, because it's an easy way to make a quick buck.

When I was in post-production on my first feature film, I needed money. I wasn't about to get a regular job working somewhere, that's just ridiculous. Instead I managed to land myself a recurring extra gig on a television show that was shooting in town. I was in three episodes, starting with the third episode of the series. The series was cancelled after the second episode aired though, so I never got my five seconds of background fame.

For those of you that may consider extra gigs in your future, allow me to give you a general breakdown before proceeding to my actual story.

Not all extra gigs are paid, and unpaid extra gigs are about the most worthless thing you could ever participate in. First of all, casting directors don't consider extra gigs to be actual acting, and the only reason to put them on your resume is if you have literally nothing else. Also, getting your big break while doing only extra work is next to impossible, so it's not wise to approach it as your ticket to the big times. At their very best, extra gigs are a decent way to network with people and a nice way to make a quick buck.

Most often you're paid a set amount for a work day, which consists of anywhere from 8 to 10 hours. On a typical set, the crews work day consists of at least 12 hours, so you're getting off easy. If you stay on set longer than that day, most companies will then pay you overtime by the hour. They'll also feed you. Sometimes the food is really good, other times...not so much.

You'll spend about 80% of your work day sitting in a holding area. I hope you brought a book, an iPod, and a couple other things to occupy your time, because it's dead boring. If they choose to use you, you'll then go to the set, be assign a series of motions (go pick up those plates and come back, walk across the street, hail a cab, that sort of thing) to repeat 6 or 7 times while they film. Then you go back to the holding area. Repeat until you go home.

It sounds amazingly glamorous doesn't it? This is the fast paced world of film, where dreams are made. There are actually people out there who make a living off of this insanely boring job, and I wish them all the success in the world. I'd kill myself.

Of course, being an extra isn't always so exciting and

delightful, which brings us to our actual story.

I'm playing an extra at an outdoor wedding. This means I'm dressed up in formal clothes. Now I HATE formal clothes. I've never understood the need to wrap ourselves in so many uncomfortable layers of clothing just to mark an occasion. The fact that I'm present and not naked should be more than enough. Even worse is the fact that this isn't a real special occasion, I'm now dressed up in my dreaded suit for a PRETEND special occasion. I know it sounds like I'm bitching a lot for a purely voluntary gig, but there's one little fact I haven't shared with you. The holding area and the scene were both outside, it was shot in Texas, and it was shot in the month of July.

For those of you who have never been outside in Texas during July, try your best to picture what life is like on the surface of the sun. Now picture that that sun is about to crash into a much larger sun. THAT'S HOW HOT IT IS IN THE SHADE!

So I'm quietly boiling away for 12 hours, in a suit. I can't even cross my arms, because that leaves HUGE sweat marks on my shirt. It is a completely miserable experience.

At the end of the day I collect my money, hop into my car, and make a very important decision. I decide to strip down naked in an attempt to cool off. I place all my clothes on the seat beside me, and begin the drive home, steam gently rising from my parboiled body.

I was actually a little concerned about getting pulled over and having to explain to the officer why I had no clothes on. But this concern was quickly overcome by another more pressing matter. I needed to pee like never before, and I was still 30 minutes from home.

There was no WAY I was putting that suit back on just so I could walk into a gas station bathroom and relieve myself. Instead, I came up with an alternative solution. There was a mostly empty Chik-fil-a cup in my car (and this is the kind of advertising they NEVER wanted). So I pulled behind a gas station, where nobody could see in the car, and made the cup significantly less empty. Wow, that was a really nice way of saying I peed into the cup.

Now I'm sitting in my car naked, holding a cup filled with my own urine. This is not acceptable. I check to make sure nobody is looking, chuck the cup out of my window, and don't look back. That's right ladies, this classy gentleman is single.

When I finally got home, I had cooled a little, but not enough to be willing to put on my suit again. I merely put on my boxers and creep into my house. My sister was in the living room watching television…man did she regret staying up late.

As my sister tried to erase the image of her mostly naked older brother from her mind, I felt a remarkable sense of déjà vu.

Many years back, I was in college, and the Gay and Lesbian Club was having a party. There was Jell-O wrestling. There was me. I was Jell-O wrestling. I would like to formally go on record now as saying that the idea of watching girls Jell-O wrestle is MUCH more satisfying than the actual act of Jell-O wrestling. Especially when your opponent is another man.

It was slippery, disgusting, but thankfully brief. In short it was almost exactly like the first time I had sex. And, just like the first time I had sex, I totally won. I feel that's an important thing to add to the story. I totally won.

Only now my clothes are literally dripping with Jell-O, and I have nice upholstered seats in my car. Only one solution I can see, throw the clothes in the trunk and drive home naked.

When I get to my apartment I decide to force my way back into my Jell-O underwear, and walk as quickly and as stealthily as possible into my apartment.

I honestly believe that the very last thing Princess EVER thought she would see in her life was me sneaking into our apartment mostly naked and covered with Jell-O. Like so many of my friends though, she didn't bother to ask any questions.

It took three showers to remove all the Jell-O from all the various places that Jell-O had decided to live. The shower looked like war crimes had been committed in it. It was horrific, so I chose to not clean it up. What's the point in creating a God-awful mess like that if you can't share it with your roommates?

This story comes to you bereft of any moral. I'm hard-pressed to even find a point to it beyond the fact that I seem to drive naked more than I think anybody reasonably should.

I thought you might like to know that.

Life with My Father

Well, I began this book by talking about my mother's inability to perform a simple function like laundry. I might as well end it by talking about my father's failures as a human being.

Before we get too far into this, I'd like to say that my father is a smart man, he has a vocabulary that has been known to flummox the ill-prepared. He's also a good and kind man. I say these things because after you finish reading this chapter, you may walk away with the wrong idea about him. And you know any time someone begins a story by defending the subject of the story, it's going to get mean.

Growing up, my dad could be a bit scary. He was always a big man, but not in a fat sort of way. Let's just say that I always won "My Dad Can Beat Up Your Dad" as a kid. He also had a pretty famous temper.

Now, let's be completely fair and honest here. My father never beat me...except once, and I totally had it coming. I also got spanked once as a kid, after shooting him in the eye with a suction dart gun, in front of a business client. I think we can all agree that I had that one coming too.

But apart from those two times I honestly deserved it, he never raised a hand to me or my sister in anger. Although he did flip a table once.

He hates this story, and has long claimed that it never happened, but some things stay etched in the brain. Besides, he also claims to have never had the "It's ok if you're gay" talk with me, which he did FIVE TIMES, so clearly he can't be trusted.

It was a Saturday, and my mother always worked on Saturdays, so when my dad went to take a nap, my sister and I were alone in the house. We made a mess, we made a very big mess. We took a completely clean room and turned it into a biohazard. We were young, it happens. When my dad awoke from his nap to see the havoc we had wrought, he was furious. He flipped a large wooden coffee table at us (to be fair, I don't think he was aiming for us, we just happened to be in that general direction) and yelled at us for a while.

Needless to say, we spent a lot of time running to our mother for permission and protection.

That changed as he got older. It's really weird. It's like one day he just woke up and decided "What's the point in getting angry all the time?" He mellowed out completely. Oh sure, he can still get angry when the situation calls for it, and it still feels very much like the wrath of God, but it rarely happens.

His temper wasn't the only thing about him that stuck with me; his way of speech has forever altered who I am as a person. He has a very loud voice. I attribute some of my volume control to growing up in the same house as him (mainly because it's always nice when we can blame our faults on other people). It's funny, because when he talks on the phone, especially long distance, he tends to speak even louder. It's almost as if he believes that the telephone company needs some extra help to get all the way to the other side of the call.

He also occasionally blanks on words. This has gotten more pronounced as he's gotten older. He'll be in the middle of a sentence, when suddenly the next word eludes him. Rather than scramble around for another word, he'll just stand there until he thinks of it. Since I've grown up with this (and terrifyingly enough, have had it happen to me as I've gotten older), I quickly supply the missing word for him. Unfortunately this has become a habit. Why is this unfortunate? When people stumble or falter on words, and you start putting words in their mouth, they rarely thank you for it. It's gotten me in trouble over the years. Even worse, I've picked up the habit too, although when I blank on a word, I don't even try to summon it up, I just gesture until someone fills it in.

My father has also never been big on communication. He's never felt a particular need to let people know what he's thinking, where he's going, or why he's suddenly decided to spend a couple hours picking up trash from the side of the road. Anytime my family has decided to go do something together, all preparations are made with an eye on my dad. We never know exactly when he's going to be ready, and nobody is going to rush him. If I had a nickel for every time a family outing starting with someone shouting "Dad's in the car! Dad's in the car!" in a panicked shout as we all start running about, I'd be a very rich man indeed. You knew you were in real trouble if the car started backing out of the driveway with nobody else in it yet.

A last word or warning for all of you. Never ask my dad for directions. Just don't. Ever. He has a great sense of direction, I've never known the man to get lost. He just uses odd reference points. Directions from my father will normally sound like this...

"Ok, remember the baseball field that you played on when you were five?"

No Dad, I don't remember a place I went a couple times when I was practically an infant.

"Well, go there and take a left. Now, a little bit further on is that hamburger place we went for your eighth birthday. It's been torn down and now it's a Wal-Mart, but take a right there."

Wait, did he really just tell me to use a place that doesn't exist, and that I wouldn't remember if it did as directions? Yes he did.

"Ok, now on your right you'll see a big tree, across the street from that is a street coming off of another street, go there."

Wait, what!? WHAT!? We're now using flora as landmarks? I swear, if he tells me to turn left at the cow I'm going to punch him in the face!

And then run away really fast, because my dad is still

a big man.

The Untold Tales

There were quite a few stories that weren't told here. Some were of a very personal nature; others were too graphic for general audiences. Some I just couldn't find enough material in to actually take the time to type out. Some, quite frankly, just weren't good enough. Here are a couple stories I didn't tell, and the reason I didn't share them.

Life In The Photo Lane – I spent a large amount of my high school and college years working in photo labs. I loved it, I had a natural gift for it. Anywhere I worked I was quickly hailed as "The Photo God" (seriously, it was on my nametag at some places). And trust me, I have tons of anecdotes related to developing other people's memories.

Why I Didn't Write It – A couple of reasons really. First, photo labs are old news at this point. Digital photography has pretty much eliminated 1-Hour Photo Labs, which makes me sad. It also makes a lot of the stories archaic to today's audiences. Plus, I'm not sure legally how much I should share. Let me say this much though, if you ever wondered if photo lab employees would occasionally make extra copies of your photos...yes, yes they did.

Princess And The Boy – I mentioned my friend Princess a couple times in this book, and she's one of my more unique friends. I love her to death, but not many other people do, nor do I expect them to. That's ok though, she doesn't usually like other people either. Also, whoever Princess is dating is always universally known as The Boy. The reason for this is long and boring. As she's so unique, I could spend quite a while writing about her.

Why I Didn't Write It – Honestly, it's just rough to turn a single character into a cohesive narrative. Plus, I think I make her sound more extreme than she really is. That, coupled with her shyness, makes me pretty sure if I did write an entire chapter about her, she wouldn't talk to me again. I value her friendship, and thus I will grant her privacy. I will share this though - her real name isn't Princess, not really. One day in our friendship she complained to me that she'd never had a nickname (apart from references to her red hair), so I thought about it long and hard. I came to the realization that I only ever felt two ways about her. Either she was being cute, adorable, and such a charming little Princess, or she was being self-centered, childish, and such a freaking little Princess. The name stuck. While she's always quick to point out to people that her name isn't really Princess, she has admitted that she likes being called one, as she never felt like one growing up.

The Abused Children's Shelter – I've mentioned working at an abused children's shelter a few times. I was there for three years, half of that time on the night shift. I have enough stories to fill a book, and get everyone I ever worked with arrested. And while there are some stories I'm very tempted to tell, I won't write them in this book, and probably not in any future books.

Why I Didn't Write It – First of all, it'd turn this into a Science Fiction book. Seriously though, some of the stories are flat out disturbing. Others are only funny because of the situation we were all in. A lot would paint the people working there in a bad light (they aren't, for the most part, they're just making the best of a hideous situation). And also, all the kids that were there had gone through great tragedies in their life. If they are ever to have happy, healthy lives, they need to move on from their pasts. If even one kid were to pick up this book, and relive this horrible time in their lives, I couldn't live with myself. Life was hard enough on these kids without me making them the butt of literary comedy.

Silently Stalking Sarah – So, through a series of events so improbable that even Douglas Adams couldn't have dreamed of them, there's a girl out there who believes I spent a good portion of my life stalking her. It's a combination of lies told to her, me being awkward talking to girls at that age, and me having a really good memory. Also I think there were aliens.

Why I Didn't Write It – Because honestly I think it would almost come across as "protesting too much." It'd be an incredibly one-sided story (although accurate) that would become of questionable veracity as it went on. Plus, it would come across as pretty whiny. I will say, in my defense, that I am WAY too lazy to actually stalk someone. I have a hard enough time finding time to spend with people who WANT to be around me. If someone doesn't want me around, I pretty much cease caring about them, there's just so much else to deal with in life. Lastly, the idea of spending an entire chapter of a book explaining that I didn't really care about a person seems pretty self-defeating. It'd be like calling someone to explain that you don't have time to talk to them. So here's the short version of the story – Sarah, I'm not stalking you, I never did, get over yourself, and I hope you have a nice life.

The Girls Of The Grocery Aisle – Is there anything more important to a teenage boy than teenage girls? My first serious job as a teenager was at a grocery store, and I was surrounded by a bevy of beauties. I was tempted to tell the tale of my attempts to woo each of them, which honestly would make a pretty decent story.

Why I Didn't Write It – A little similar to the story above honestly. The idea of spending a lot of time and effort writing about a bunch of girls I had a crush on as a teenager seems a little worrisome. Also, since I utterly and spectacularly failed to woo any of them, it'd make me look pretty pathetic. I think I've looked pathetic enough through the course of this book, I'm not going to add to it. Although, I'm thinking of taking my entire experience working at that store (particularly about the girls) and writing a coming of age style film about it. It's got potential.

Brushes With Fame – Working in the film industry, I've occasionally met some celebrities. Who doesn't like celebrity gossip? I could name names, tell you what they're like in person. That sort of thing.

Why I Didn't Write It – Because it's stupid. I've never understood the fascination with celebrities. All of them are just people doing a job, why do so many people care more about what a celebrity does than what happens in their own life? I honestly do not get it. Now, the first time I had a conversation with a celebrity, I was nervous as hell. I was only used to seeing her on the big screen, having her in the same room with me was odd, but I got over that after I accidently saw her naked. She didn't catch me, but it brought home the fact that people are just people, no matter what the job description. If I were to spend an entire chapter name-dropping, I'd be just as bad as everyone who watches TMZ. I will drop just one name though, because it was very Jeff of me. I did manage to piss off Jon Voight, but I swear it wasn't really my fault, really! And no matter what anyone tells you, I DID NOT ask him for his daughter's phone number. That's an outright lie.

Hot Nuns – The story of the time I single-handedly prevented a bus full of nuns from crashing into a bus full of supermodels. Both buses were very grateful. The nuns even forgave the sinful way I received thanks from the models

Why I Didn't Write It – The main reason I didn't write this story, despite it perhaps being the best story ever, is that it didn't happen. No part of it, in any permutation. It is entirely fictional.

Terrorizing Teachers – I spent a lot of my time in school irritating teachers. It wasn't always on purpose, but sometimes it was. Most often this was because I wanted to understand things better than they were explaining, so I'd ask a lot of "why?" questions. Nothing irritates people more than "why?" questions, because they're the hardest to answer. I will defend to my death that I was well within my rights as a student to press my teachers for answers to questions. The more they avoided answering, the harder I'd press. But sometimes, I was just being a dick.

Why I Didn't Write It – Because I don't want to encourage kids to be dicks to teachers. Teachers have it pretty rough as it is. That said though, I still think it's important to ask questions. I think it's the best way to understand something. Never be afraid to ask questions. And, let me give you one answer that my first grade teacher NEVER gave me, and that I learned myself when I was much older. The reason you're colouring in a stupid balloon for 20 minutes is because the classroom is full of noisy children and the teacher would like a few moments to hear her own thoughts.

Epilogue: My Life's Groovy

I had a bit of a personal revelation the other day. In the process of gathering stories for this book, I spent a lot of time looking back over my life, trying to figure out how I went so horribly awry, and then I realized: my life ain't so bad. True, I'm 28 years old and live with my parents. Sure I have absolutely no romantic prospects. True, I don't, at the moment, have viable reliable income. True, I'm a bit overweight (I prefer to think of myself as stocky; it paints a more accurate picture). True, I haven't made my bed in well over a year (I still wash sheets, just throw them back on afterward). True, all of these previous facts bother me from time to time (except the bed one, because seriously, why spend time doing something I'll undo later that evening?). But because of a slovenly angel I met the other day, I know my life ain't that bad.

I may have briefly touched on my high school years. I wasn't the most popular. I had plenty of friends, but I didn't belong to any clique, which was necessary for popularity. Mind you, popularity was never really a goal of mine, and cliques have never had an appeal to me.

Cliques are like reverse racism to me. Racism is taking a look at a whole group of people with one trait in common, and painting them all as bad, or less than you. Joining a clique is looking at a group of people with one trait in common (membership in the clique) and saying that they are equal to you. Both are pretty stupid. Say what you will about Muslims, or homosexuals, or Republicans, or Democrats, or Scientologists, or even Furries, but all of those groups are comprised of individuals. To judge an entire group is the purest form of laziness. Within that group you'll find all types of people, some good, some bad.

I've always preferred to dislike people for who they are, not what they say or believe. So yeah, I had some friends in the band, and some in the drama club, and some jocks, and even a couple of cheerleaders. But, those that weren't my friends had a pretty low opinion of me. I was weird, a freak, an outcast. I didn't belong to any group, so I was shunned by most of them. This probably should have bothered me, but it didn't. I had friends; they accepted me for who I was. What more does a person really need than that?

So the picture I'm trying to paint for you is one of mild teasing and scorn, but nothing that landed me in therapy, or had me packing a Glock to school (although there were rumours). Those that were popular certainly had much easier lives than I did. Most of them came from money too. It was a frequent game at my school to go out after Christmas and count the number of new Mustangs. It was always in the double digits. My family has always been pretty solidly middle class. That's never bothered me, we never wanted for anything. It was just another thing to set me apart from my peers.

I ended up going to college about 30 miles from my high school. It was a good college, and had a great film program. I even ran into a couple people I went to high school with there. It wasn't until a semester or two later that the most amazing thing happened. The number of students at my university that I went to high school with quadrupled.

They all had the same story to tell too. They left our little bubble of a school district to go out into the scary world. Suddenly they were in another state, at another school, and nobody gave a crap about them. Nobody cared that they were popular in high school, nobody cared if their parents had money. Nobody cared what cliques they had belonged to. So many of them suffered from such severe culture shock that after a semester or two they moved back home, and transferred to my college.

It was always kind of funny to me. I'd see these people who would have never spoken a kind word to me in high school, and the second they saw me their faces would light up. "You knew me in high school," their eyes would say "you remember that I was important." Now, a bitter man, a cynical man abused by life, would have told them to go pound sand (an expression my father really enjoys). But I wasn't scarred by my high school experiences. So I'd great them with joy, and even act a little bit like I was lucky they were deigning to speak with me. It was the least I could do, these guys were just coasting through life when reality slammed on the breaks. Me, I was used to driving with the emergency brake on.

Now, some of you may think I'm getting a bit off track here, and you'd be wrong. "But Jeff, what about the slovenly angel, and the personal revelation?" I hear you ask. I'm getting there, just relax and enjoy the ride man. I don't come to your job and tell you what pace to work at.

After graduating I've had almost zero contact with anyone I went to high school with. I occasionally talk to a girl I've been friends with since Kindergarten, and another guy I've been friends with since the fifth grade, but that's it. The other day I ran into a gas station to buy a last-second lottery ticket, and the guy mopping the floor in his wrinkled jumpsuit looked familiar to me.

Oh man, I went to high school with this guy. He wasn't uberpopular, but he certainly had an easier time of it than me. Here he is mopping the floor of a gas station not ten minutes drive from our old high school. Please don't let him recognize me. Please don't let him recognize me.

And then he called out my name. I acted happy to see him to, in reality I felt guilty. I was dressed in some of my best casual clothes (new jeans, white t-shirt, fancy button down shirt open on top, I looked GOOD), and unlike him, I didn't seem to have the weight of the world on my shoulders.

I opened with "Hey man, how's it going?" He simply looked at himself, and at the mop, and said "you can see how it's going." Wow, ok, it's going to be like that. I told him I don't judge, and for all he knew I was working at the gas station down the street. He said the one down street was a lot nicer than the one he worked in. Damn, he's determined to make me feel guilty for not sucking.

Then he asked me what I was doing for a living.

I should have lied. I should have said I scrape road-kill off the road. This guy was making me feel guilty for not being miserable. Instead, I did as I so often do in a panicked situation, I told the truth. I told him I was a filmmaker who was writing a book. He seemed really happy for me, but that weight on his shoulders had just increased. You could almost hear him thinking "how is this dweeb from high school happy with his life? How am I here?"

I tried to cheer him up, I told him that I was living with my parents. He told me he was too, and his dad was dying of cancer.

At that moment I decided that he had won, my life was officially awesome. We chatted a bit about the upcoming 10-year reunion, and then I hit the bricks, vowing never to go inside that gas station again.

It'd be different if he'd been mean to me in high school, but I don't recall him being any crueler than anyone else. It was just amazing to me to see how someone could coast through their teenage years, and then when confronted with reality, they never recover.

Let me leave you with this bit of advice, because it's important information to have.

First, to those of you who don't fit in. Those who view themselves as outcasts, or undesirables, or whatever term is hip today, life isn't always like that. I mean it. The first day you set foot in college, you'll realize that you're in a place where individuality is celebrated. It's there that you really get to let your freak flag fly (as the cool kids say.)

You take the classes you're interested in, which means you're surrounded by people interested in the same thing. There is NOBODY so unique that there aren't at least 20 other people just like them on any college campus. Until then, just stay under the radar, do your time, and wait until freedom. I know telling you to tone it down seems like bad advice, but if your individuality is causing your life to be a living hell in high school, just tone it down temporarily. It doesn't seem like it now, but high school is such a tiny blip on the radar of your life, seriously.

Now, for all the popular kids who cost through school on good lucks, charm, money, and whatever else it takes to be popular. Enjoy it while you can. I mean that seriously, enjoy it, but know that it ends. Eventually the ride gets bumpy, and it takes work to keep going. Be ready for that day, it's coming sooner than you want to think. And lastly, before you pick on that weird freak, remember it's computer nerds who become billionaires, and drama dweebs who become celebrities. Adversity tends to create the artistic types that succeed in our world. In the long run, it's probably better to be nice to them, or at least leave them alone. I mean think about it, do you really want to be the guy who bullied the next Johnny Depp and then ended up spending your life working at a fast food restaurant? Is that a chance you're comfortable taking?

Both sides need to keep in mind that the future contains a lot more time than the past. The things you're doing today likely won't matter at all to you 30 years from now.

To plagiarize an expression from a Canadian comedy show, The Red Green Show, I'm pulling for you, we're all in this together.

Thank you so much for coming with me on this journey through my past. It turned out to be surprisingly therapeutic for me, and hopefully it was a little entertaining for you. After reading all of these stories, you probably know me as well as some of my closest friends. I won't make some big cheesy story about how you're now a dear, dear friend to me, but I have nothing but fondness in my heart for you, after making it through all of this. Thank you again.

I will finish by saying that the events you have read about are 100% true, as I remember them. If you were to track down the people from this book, they'd probably tell things a little differently, but it's the nature of reality to be subjective.

If you enjoyed these stories, tell a friend. If you hated them, tell an enemy.

ABOUT THE AUTHOR

Jeff Hillary is a native Texan, and wouldn't have it any other way. He graduated from the University of North Texas with a degree in film and currently lives in Austin. He can often be found in the company of the misfits he is lucky enough to call his friends.

He also enjoys Sunkist, his foo-foo-girly dog, and would probably like long walks on the beach, if he ever actually visited a beach.

Made in the USA
Columbia, SC
22 October 2021

47637730R00146